A TEENAGER
IN HITLER'S
DEATH CAMPS

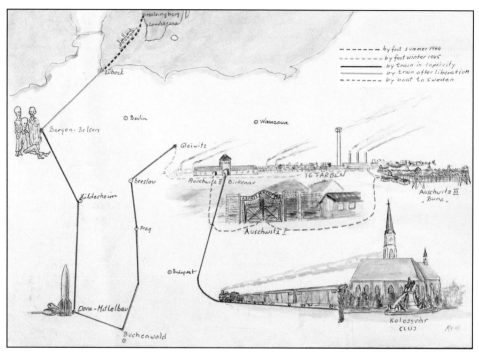

This map traces my route from my hometown of Kolozsvar, which today is in Romania, to Sweden. During the Second World War, I was taken to various concentration camps in Poland and Germany. After the war was over, I was brought to Sweden along with other sick camp inmates.

A TEENAGER
IN HITLER'S
DEATH CAMPS

BENNY GRÜNFELD

IN COLLABORATION WITH

MAGNUS HENREKSON

AND

OLLE HÄGER

TRANSLATED BY

KEN SCHUBERT

BENBELLA BOOKS, INC.

DALLAS, TEXAS

First BenBella Books Edition August 2007

BenBella Books, Inc.
6440 N. Central Expressway, Suite 617
Dallas, TX 75206
www.benbellabooks.com
Send feedback to feedback@benbellabooks.com

Printed in China
10 9 8 7 6 5 4 3 2 1

Library of Congress Cataloging-in-Publication Data

Grünfeld, Benny.
  [Tonåring i Hitlers dödsläger. English]
  A teenager in Hitlers death camps / Benny Grunfeld in collaboration with Magnus Henrekson and Olle Häger ; translated by Ken Schubert.—1st BenBella Books ed.
    p. cm.
  ISBN 1-933771-19-4
  1. Grünfeld, Benny. 2. Jews—Romania—Cluj-Napoca—Biography. 3. Jewish children in the Holocaust—Romania—Cluj-Napoca—Biography. 4. Holocaust, Jewish (1939-1945)—Romania—Cluj-Napoca—Personal narratives. 5. Holocaust survivors—Sweden—Biography. 6. Cluj-Napoca (Romania)—Biography. I. Henrekson, Magnus. II. Häger, Olle. III. Title.

  DS135.R73G782413 2007
  940.53'18092—dc22

  [B]

                                                                                  2006100195

Proofreading by Emily Chauviere and Sean Sweeney
Cover design by Laura Watkins
Text design and composition by John Reinhardt Book Design
Printed by C & C Offset Printing Co., Ltd.

Distributed by Independent Publishers Group
To order call (800) 888-4741
www.ipgbook.com

For media inquiries and special sales contact Yara Abuata at yara@benbellabooks.com

In remembrance of my parents, Regina and Josef,
and my little brother Alexander

CONTENTS

FOREWORD

THIS IS MY EYEWITNESS ACCOUNT of the Holocaust, the most heinous crime in human history.

My story is addressed particularly to today's high school and junior high school students. I myself was sixteen years old when our family was swept away in evil's deluge.

Here I am at the age of seventeen. Sixty-one years have passed since this picture was taken in a Swedish photo studio. That's a long time. But I haven't forgotten my experiences in the camps, everything I witnessed with my own eyes.

Herman, I, and our eldest brother Armand are sitting between my mother and my uncle. I am the smallest. The photo was taken when I was two years old. Alexander was not yet born.

A SHORT FAMILY
BIOGRAPHY

MY FATHER JOSEF and his twin brother Jacob were the second youngest in a family of five boys and two girls. Jacob, his older sister Anna, and his oldest brother Farkas all lived in the U.S. My father planned to go there as soon as persecution of the Jews had become too intense. But he never made it, either because he didn't have enough money or because it was difficult for Jews to get entry visas to the U.S.

His brother Samuel died of tuberculosis at the age of twenty-five, before the war broke out. My father, Jacob, and their next oldest brother, Marton, were all watchmakers. Since their youngest sister Serena lived in the Romanian part of Transylvania, she was never deported to the extermination camps.

My father was educated at Glashütte, the famous German watch-making school. We boys looked up to him. He was well-known for his craftsmanship; in his free time he played the violin, and even played billiards once in a while. But he devoted most of his time to his family. Despite the hard times, we never went hungry. I can't remember him ever taking a vacation.

My mother's name was Regina, but everyone called her Pippi. She was twenty-five when she married my father, who was forty at the time. When we were deported, she was forty-six. She was the second youngest in a family of six girls and two boys. Only one of her brothers, who lived in Romanian Transylvania, escaped deportation. Two of my cousins on my mother's side survived the war. One of them was killed immediately afterwards in a laboratory explosion in France.

My mother's mother became a widow at an early age; she was left all alone with eight children. Her husband had been a kosher butcher. His knife slipped one day, and he cut himself so badly that he died of

My mother and father

blood poisoning. I don't remember him, but I remember my grand-mother as clearly as can be. She was a thoroughly good person. She and her only unmarried daughter Duna managed to live on the widow's pension the Jewish congregation gave her. Though there were several men who wanted to marry her, Duna decided to stay with her mother. Though the camp authorities chose her to perform slave labor, she voluntarily followed her mother into the gas chamber.

My oldest brother, Armand, was five years older than I. He was a very talented child and always got top grades in school. He started to play the violin at the age of six. When he was twelve, he began to build radio receivers. He was one of the few Jews who were allowed to continue their education after high school. The Jews' enemies tried to keep us out of colleges and universities. He got into a trade college. Actually, he wanted to go to a technical college, but the Jewish

My grandmother Marika, seated, and my mother's siblings Malka, Moshe, and Duna. My grandmother and both of my mother's sisters were killed at Auschwitz.

quota had already been filled. In March 1944 he was drafted into the army. That turned out to be the best thing that could have happened to him. Several weeks later the Germans occupied Hungary; if he hadn't been drafted, he would have been deported to Auschwitz. During the last six months of the war, he wound up at the Dachau

My father, left, and his brothers Farkas, Marton, and Jacob. Jacob and Farkas emigrated to the U.S. in 1924.

concentration camp, which was finally liberated by the Americans. For a year after the war he played the violin in a German symphony orchestra, then emigrated to the U.S. During the 1950s he earned his university degree as a physics major. He worked for many years at RCA as a product developer, and was department head at Hughes Industries in California at the time of his retirement.

My younger brother Alexander, whom everybody called "Sanyi" (short for Sandor, the Hungarian form of Alexander), looked like me, only more handsome. Nobody could resist his charm and cheerful personality. I was often envious of him. He was also artistically gifted. I especially remem-

Alexander

ber the beautiful clay pottery he molded with his bare hands. Like me, he would turn to our grandmother when he needed to be comforted. Even after more than sixty years, I still grieve for him.

My next oldest brother, Herman, who survived the war along with me, was four years older than I. My father did not earn enough money for him to continue his education as Armand did. He was apprenticed to a goldsmith at the age of fourteen. Unfortunately, the goldsmith was excessively strict. During his frequent outbursts, he would box Herman on the ears and hit him with his tools. To be fair, I should mention that he abused his own son in the same way. My father often considered ending Herman's apprenticeship, but never did. The master was known for his skill, and his students usually became accomplished goldsmiths themselves.

Herman tried to make up for the education he had missed by buying good books with his savings. When he noticed Armand's success with the girls—largely because of his skill on the violin—he decided, at the age of seventeen, to learn to play as well. He was so intent on playing that he taught himself in record time. Soon he was just as popular with the girls as Armand. He also had the advantage of being very handsome, with thick, curly hair.

Herman

After four years as an apprentice, Herman received his master craftsman's certificate. His final piece of jewelry before we were sent to the camps, a woman's silver ring with inlaid jewels, won second prize in a major national competition in which forty journeymen from a number of different handicrafts participated. (A cabinet maker won first prize with a miniature furniture suite.) Later a local count bought the ring.

Soon after his arrival in Sweden in 1945, Herman began to work for a goldsmith in the town of Landskrona in southern Sweden. After a couple of years he moved to Stockholm and started his own workshop where he both crafted and sold the jewelry he made. However, working as a goldsmith did not satisfy Herman's artistic longings fully, so he began to study the violin and voice. He was also very active in the Jewish congregation in Stockholm.

It was eventually painting that became the medium through which he could let out his feelings and creativity. In 1988 Herman, his wife, and their four-year-old son left Sweden for Toronto in Canada, where he continues to paint. He has had numerous exhibitions in both Sweden and Canada.

Herman also has a daughter, Nava Grünfeld, born in the late 1940s in Stockholm. She and her mother, Herman's first wife, emigrated to the United States in the mid-1950s. Nava is a professional artist, best known for her bold, color-saturated watercolor paintings of still life objects.

"ONLY WHAT YOU CAN CARRY"

MARCH 19, 1944, was a dark day for me and my fellow Hungarian Jews. For most Jews living in the country-side, it meant the beginning of the Holocaust. It was the day German troops streamed into Hungary.

It took them only a few days to reach my hometown of Kolozsvar, the main city in Transylvania. Today it's called Cluj and is in Roma-nia.

With the German invasion, the forces of evil began to grow bolder. The Hungarian Nazi sympathizers ("arrowcross") carried banners on the streets and shouted slogans, all variations on the theme "Death to the Jews!" They harassed and assaulted people of Jewish descent, as well as Christians who happened to look Jewish.

Germans living in Hungary, whose families had lived in the area for generations, began to show a master-race mentality. Many of them enlisted in the German SS (the Nazi Party's elite troops, whose duties included directing the Gestapo secret police and running the con-centration camps). Young people formed Hitler Youth Groups and marched through the streets of the town wearing swastika armbands and singing Nazi songs.

[OPPOSITE, TOP]: *Our family before the Hungarian police and gendarmes led us away from our homes. My father is in his hat and overcoat. I'm standing immediately to his left. To his right stand my younger brother Alexander, my mother Regina, and my older brother Herman.*

Just as we are ordered to march off, a childless Christian woman from our block steals her way up to one of our Jewish neighbors, a mother of five children. "Let me take care of the youngest one, you're going to have your hands full with the other children," she says.

With tears in her eyes, the mother hands over her youngest child to the Christian woman, who hastily retreats carrying the child bundled in a shawl. The whole thing takes only a few seconds, but the child's life has been saved (the mother and her children were sent directly to the gas chamber upon their arrival at the Auschwitz-Birkenau extermination camp).

[OPPOSITE, BOTTOM]: *My brightest childhood memory—the day my father takes me and my young-er brother Alexander to a fun-fair that visits our home town.*

Laws and decrees depriving us Jews of our rights followed one after the other. These regulations were direct translations of the "Nuremberg Laws" that had been passed by the Nazis in Germany. The first decree required us to wear a large yellow Star of David sewn to our coats whenever we were outside.

A month after the German invasion, someone knocked on our front door early one morning. My mother opened it to find a plainclothes Hungarian policeman standing there. He told her in a gruff voice, "You must be out on the street in exactly one hour. Take along things you absolutely need for life at a camp—cooking equipment and clothing—but only what you can carry."

I could see the terror and anxiety on my parents' faces. We had hoped that we would somehow escape the horrors of the war, as well as the persecution that other Jews had suffered at the hands of the Germans. Knowing that the war was starting to go against the Germans, we had prayed that the Soviet Army would arrive in time to liberate us.

Besides me, my family consisted of my mother Regina, my father Josef, and my three brothers. My father was a watchmaker. He had been trained at Glashütte, one of Germany's most well-known vocational schools.

Armand, my oldest brother, had been drafted to the Hungarian army for labor service. That turned out to be a blessing in disguise—he escaped deportation with the rest of us. Though he eventually wound up at the Dachau concentration camp anyway, he was liberated by the Americans and later went to the U.S.

Herman, age nineteen, was my next oldest brother; he had just passed the test to become a goldsmith. His vocational training was later to save both his life and mine.

I had just turned sixteen.

My younger brother Alexander—Sanyi for short—was thirteen. My grief for him and my parents is still hard to bear, despite the fact that over fifty years have passed since we were separated upon arriving at a Nazi extermination camp in Poland. Maybe it would have been easier for me if there at least had been a gravesite to visit.

By the time we came out to the street, several hundred Jews were already there. Armed police, as well as gendarmes in ridiculous-looking hats with cock feathers, stood there waiting to lead us away.

Thus, the Holocaust began for us as we marched out of our hometown of Kolozsvar. Other groups of Jews, all guarded by Hungarian police, joined us along the way. Eventually there were several thousand of us.

They took us to an abandoned brick factory outside the city. We had to live in long rectangular drying barns, wooden buildings with brick roofs and no walls. My family was assigned a tiny corner. We had neither cots nor mattresses. We slept with only a thin layer of straw between us and the ground. The former brick factory was now a ghetto surrounded by a double barbed-wire fence and guarded by Hungarian soldiers.

Several days later they ordered us to turn in all of our valuables. Anyone who refused to obey could be executed. My father, who was a jeweler as well as a watchmaker, had given my mother a lovely wedding ring. Now she was forced to hand over her most prized possession.

Trying to prepare himself for the difficult times ahead, Herman had melted down a small quantity of gold and hidden it under the heels of his shoes. But my mother insisted that he remove the heels and hand over his modest savings to the Hungarian soldiers.

One day the authorities called for volunteers to work outside the ghetto. Herman and I both signed up, mostly for a little change of pace; it was very depressing to be cooped up in the ghetto day after day. After taking us to a match factory next to the freight yard, they ordered us to unload wooden logs. Since the guards weren't keeping close watch on us, I decided to sneak into the city and get some of the groceries we had left behind in our apartment when we were forced to leave so hurriedly and unexpectedly. I asked an older man to tell Herman that I had gone to town to pick up some food. The man turned out to be a doctor and owner of a private hospital. He asked me to stop by the hospital and tell the janitor to get together some food for him. I waited until there were no guards in sight and slipped away from the factory area.

I made it all the way to town without arousing suspicion. The first thing I did was go to the hospital and give the message to the janitor. I told him that I would come back in an hour to pick up the food. When I got to our apartment, I discovered that the authorities had sealed the door. But that didn't stop me; I had crawled in through the kitchen window many times when nobody was at home. Before you could count to ten, I was inside our empty apartment. I grabbed a little of everything that looked edible, including a bottle of the schnapps my father liked to sip after a long workday. Just as I was about to leave the apartment, our next-door neighbor showed up. She was amazed to see me; pulling me quickly into her apartment, she started to ask me questions. I had always thought she was a nice person, though I wasn't sure how much I could trust her.

I explained to her that I had volunteered to work outside the ghetto and that I had convinced the guards to let me come here and pick up a few things. That was a little white lie to keep her out of trouble if I got caught later. She asked me to wait a minute, then went out and brought me a big smoked sausage. Then I went back to the hospital and picked up some milk and other groceries from the janitor. Now I had a whole lot to carry. I hid most of it under a haystack near the workplace. That way I avoided drawing attention to myself. When I returned to work, the only thing I had was the bottle of schnapps. The doctor immediately asked me how things had gone, and I told him where I had hidden everything.

As soon as there were no guards around, we sneaked over to the haystack. Just as we were about to take the groceries, a tall Hungarian soldier walked up. He had seen me returning with the groceries from his window in the little guard house; afterwards he just sat there and waited for me to come back for them. He started beating up the innocent doctor. The doctor was over fifty and rather small; he staggered backwards after every blow. I was trembling with fright that I would be next. But the guard just bawled me out and ordered me to go back to work. I returned to the ghetto that evening with nothing to show for my adventure except a bottle of schnapps.

After we had been there for a couple of weeks, rumors began to circulate that they were going to transfer us. A high-ranking Hungarian officer arrived at the ghetto. Standing on a wooden box, he announced that they would take us in groups of 4,000 to the western bank of the Danube River, where we would do farming.

The deportation of the Jewish population from our region was facilitated by the fact that anti-Jewish sentiments were common, and with the spread of the Nazi ideology these sentiments grew increasingly intense. Two painful incidents from my childhood years give a vivid illustration of the situation.

My father worked alone in his watchmaker's workshop, so therefore he asked me from a very young age to run errands for him. Toward the end of the 1930s, when I was ten or eleven years old, I was sent to the tax authority to pay my father's taxes. A couple of tax officials looked at me scornfully and one of them remarked ironically, "So, the wicked little Jew has decided to unburden his conscience a little by giving up some of his iniquitous earnings. I am sure that he should have paid much more. We ought to eliminate the Jewish parasites." Another official then asked him if he meant that I should be eliminated too. "No, not yet," he said. "I think he deserves to grow a little bit bigger before we take him out." These horrid words were followed by a burst of laughter. The extent of their spite and hatred was so enormous that the incident is still very much with me today, almost seventy years later.

Another terrible episode took place after the Hungarian invasion of our region, i.e., after September 1941. Outside a building that looked like a theater I saw a group of gentlemen dressed up in their best Sunday clothes. Inside there were many people gathered for a political rally. I sneaked in to have a look. I was dismayed to hear them discussing how "the Jewish pack" could be exterminated, and how the Hungarian takeover and the alliance between Hungary and Nazi Germany provided a golden opportunity to once and for all get rid of all Jews. Hitler was hailed as their great hero, and the speakers that followed excelled in throwing curses against Jews. The last speaker I dared listen to before I fled in panic shouted, "We have to kill all the Jews before it's too late! No Jew will survive, that is my holy promise to you!" Loud cheering and rounds of applause were ringing in my ears as I removed myself from the theater. As soon as I was out of sight I started running. When I came home I was completely distraught with fright and anxiety. I did not mention any of this to my parents—they were overburdened by worries already.

Thus, it was clear that we could not count on help from the local population. I only know of one Jew from my hometown who avoided deportation as a result of intervention by local officials. In Cluj there was a private hospital named after its Jewish owner Matyas (Matthew in English). He was also unique in that his first and last names were identical. He was both loved and admired, despite being a Jew, because he was an exceptionally skilled surgeon. His fame reached far outside of Cluj. His diagnoses were impeccable and his skill with the surgeon's knife bordered on wizardry. He was also kind and generous, and it was common knowledge that he often refrained from collecting his fee when a patient was of poor means. This man's unselfishness and righteousness were so great that they literally saved his life.

My grandmother and my aunt Duna get ready to climb into a freight car for deportation from Kolozsvar.
A woman who survived the camps told us later that the doctor on the platform at Auschwitz-Birkenau offered my aunt the chance to go to the right—in other words, to do slave labor—but that she preferred to follow her mother into the gas chamber.

The convoys began the following morning. The day after, it was our turn to march to the Kolozsvar train station. When we got there, the military officer loudly ordered us into freight cars.

There were 100 people in each freight car. At one end of the car we had a bucket in which to relieve ourselves. The journey was one long nightmare. It was crowded and hot. They gave us neither food nor water. The stench from the bucket was almost unbearable.

After a day or so, we could glimpse station names through tiny openings in the corners of the freight car. It was now obvious that we weren't heading west at all, but rather north toward Czechoslovakia and Poland. I could see the fright in the eyes of my father and other adults. Benjamin Buxbaum, my old elementary school principal, was in our car, and I noticed fright in his face as well. He mumbled Hebrew prayers nearly the whole time. I knew that he had a daughter living in Prague. Since the Jews there had been among the first to be deported, he was no doubt aware of what was going to happen to us.

It is sunrise, and our train has just pulled into Auschwitz-Birkenau. The doctor, who is wearing an officer's uniform, asks my father if Alexander and I are twins. He asks in a friendly tone of voice, as if he has taken a personal interest in us. When my father answers that we are almost three years apart, the doctor points Alexander to the left and me to the right.

Only long afterwards did I realize why my father had been asked upon our arrival at Auschwitz whether Alexander and I were twins. The unknown camp doctor, who turned out to be Josef Mengele, conducted brutal research on pairs of twins. He subjected them to all kinds of medical experiments before finally killing them by injecting chloroform directly into their hearts, causing their blood to congeal. Autopsies were performed right there in the camp; the most essential organs were preserved and sent to Berlin for additional research. The Hungarian-Jewish doctor Miklos Nyiszli describes this research in his book Auschwitz: A Doctor's Eyewitness Account *(Panther Books, 1962). A skillful pathologist, Dr. Nyiszli managed to survive Auschwitz by performing autopsies on the twins used by Dr. Mengele in his experiments.*

TO HELL ON EARTH

AFTER WE HAD been confined to the freight car for four days and nights, the doors finally opened. The sun was just rising, and we encountered a nightmarish scene: live barbed-wire fences, inmates in striped uniforms, armed guards with German shepherds. We had come to the Auschwitz-Birkenau extermination camp in Poland.

Even before getting off the train, we heard shrill, impatient shouts: "Women and children over here!" "Men all together!" Command after command. Suddenly my mother was separated from us. It all happened in the bat of an eyelash. Then she was gone. We didn't even have time to say good-bye. She vanished, whisked away by the guards—and I was never to see her again.

They led my father, my two brothers, and me to a courteous, uniformed doctor. Pointing to me and to my younger brother Alexander, he asked if we were twins. My father, who spoke German, answered truthfully that Alexander was thirteen and that I had just turned sixteen. The doctor then gestured that I was to go to the right, Alexander to the left. My brother Herman was directed to the right, my father to the left.

Herman and I to the right. My father and Alexander to the left. It was all decided right then and there. Going to the left meant the gas chamber.

An inmate led us into the camp. Torah scrolls were scattered along the road. Cold shivers ran down my spine when I saw our most holy scripture, so sacred that it may not be touched by human hands, lying like rubbish in the mud and filth. Instinctively, I bent down and picked up a little prayer book, which was to be my constant companion and consolation from that time on. I decided to hide it in one of my shoes, and since it was so tiny, there was actually room for it there.

After being taken to a large barn, we were ordered to undress, except for our shoes and waist belt. Next a group of inmates gave us crew cuts and cut off all our bodily hair. The scissors were blunt, and it hurt when they yanked on the hair. When they were through, they took us to another building, where they smeared us with a corrosive liquid disinfectant. Although we showered immediately afterwards, our skin smarted for several days. The building that housed the showers was located close to the crematorium.

There was a picket fence in the back of the building. Through the chinks we could see a steam shovel digging enormous pits. Later we discovered that the Germans burned bodies in the pits.

However, the crematorium didn't have the capacity to burn the bodies of all the Jews who arrived each day from Hungary and other parts of Europe to be gassed to death.

At that time, the summer of 1944, more people were killed daily in Auschwitz-Birkenau than ever before. The pits were the worst fate a Jew could suffer. One by one they were brought forward, shot in the back of the head with a small-bore revolver and slung into the fiery pit while still struggling for life. Occasionally the SS officers threw a child into the pit without even shooting him. Smoke from the crematorium and the pits constantly wafted through the camp. We were plagued day and night by the nauseating odor of burning flesh. We had obviously come to hell on Earth.

When we were finished showering, they led us to an area called C Camp. Birkenau was surrounded on all sides by a live barbed-wire fence. On the other side of the fence were deep ditches and watchtowers with armed sentries.

Our barrack in C Camp was one of hundreds of virtually identical wooden buildings, each of which could house approximately a

---

Our food rations were diabolically calculated. The daily ration was approximately 500 calories, which meant that it took three months at the most for an inmate who had been assigned to hard labor to shrivel to skin and bones.

Those inmates who, due to undernourishment, could no longer work regular shifts died in the camp hospital. Some inmates committed suicide by throwing themselves onto the live barbed-wire fence that surrounded the camp.

When the group to which Herman and I have been assigned grows to thirty men, an inmate comes and leads us into the camp. We pass right by a heap of prayer books and Torah scrolls, strewn helter-skelter all over the place to further humiliate us. Of the approximately 4,000 Jews who had been deported to Auschwitz-Birkenau in our train, only thirty-four men and a few women made it through the doctor's elimination process. For the time being, they would let us survive as slave laborers.

The image of the holy scriptures has left a permanent impression on me, along with the image of the SS officers sitting in the Mercedes convertible.

thousand inmates. Instead of beds, we had rectangular cots, stacked three high. Ten people lying back to back could fit in one cot. But if one person wanted to turn around, everyone else had to do so at the same time. There wasn't even straw to lie on, only rough planks. The people on the bottom cot had the worst time of it, since they lay directly on the ground.

Within the camp itself, everything was run by inmates. The SS officers entered the camp only for executions, inspections, and body searches when we returned from work in the evenings. A frightful kind of egoism was the rule, and the privileged inmates were extraordinarily brutal toward us ordinary inmates. The highest posts were reserved for German criminals, Aryans, "ethnic Germans" (who had been living in other countries), Polish Christians, etc. On the next

On our very first day at the camp, the authorities choose me for the gas chamber. Luckily, I later manage to slip away from the group and hide in a latrine until it starts to get dark.

rung down in the hierarchy were the assistants, who could be of any one of several nationalities. Most people on these two levels quickly learned to "suck upward and kick downward" without the least hesitation. Thanks to the fact that Herman was so useful to our "capo," the inmate put in charge of the rest of us by the camp administration, we both received certain privileges.

Each barrack had a *Blockältester* (barrack captain). Under him were three or four *Stubendienst* (barrack assistants), whose duties included helping maintain order during the distribution of food. Most of the barrack captains and assistants would strike us with their clubs at the least provocation, especially when there were SS officers around.

After we had been in the barrack for an hour, they ordered us back out and told us to line up at arm-length intervals so an SS sergeant could inspect us. He addressed us briefly: "You have come to a German concentration camp, and you will work here as long as your strength permits. After that there's only one way out, and that's through the chimney." With a smug expression on his face, he pointed toward the smoking chimney of the crematorium. Since he was standing directly in front of me, I could read the words on his belt: *Gott mit uns* (God is with us). The first thought that crossed my mind was that there was no way God could be with those bastards.

As I stood there, I had a horrible feeling in my chest. I was in physical pain and having difficulty breathing, I was fully convinced that this spot where the Hungarian fascists had brought us would be our death. It seemed especially unfair that we would be executed without anyone ever finding out about it. What had we done to deserve such a cruel death in this foreign country? I desperately hoped that at least one of us would escape and tell the world—at least the people who weren't entirely indifferent—what had happened.

The sergeant inspected us one by one. When my turn came, he gave me the sign to step to the side and join the group that was to be split off from the others. Herman was to remain with the first group. Though I had no way of knowing that my group was marked for the gas chamber, I was depressed and frightened that I would be separated from my only remaining brother. I decided right then and there not to obey the order, regardless of the consequences.

When we were children, our favorite game was hide-and-seek. Since I grew up during the rough times of the 1930s, my father had to work hard just to scrape up money for food and rent, and I can't remember ever having any toys. But I was always good at hide-and-seek, and that saved my life.

As soon as I was sure that the SS sergeant and the barrack assistants no longer had their eyes on me, I started to slip away from the rest of the group, inch by inch. Quick as a wink, I slunk around the corner of the barrack and along the wall into a building that had been fixed up as a latrine. I huddled in a corner of the latrine until it began to get dark, then made my way into my brother's barrack without anyone noticing me. Some inmates from our hometown told me where Herman's cot was. We were overjoyed to see each other again.

Later in the evening, we ate our first meal at the camp. After ordering us to line up, barrack assistants led us to the barrack captain's room, where we each received a quarter loaf of bread. As soon as we returned to our cots, we heard a terrible brawl in the barrack captain's room. The reason for the commotion was that there had been no bread left when they got to the last inmate. They had realized that there must be an inmate in the barrack who didn't belong there.

The search for the impostor began immediately. I was scared to death as I watched the barrack assistants go from cot to cot with their flashlights. Pressing up against the wall, I tried to make myself as tiny as possible. Since I was far younger than anyone else in our group, it would have been easy to identify me as the culprit. But after searching for a long time, they gave up, most likely because the barrack captain didn't dare report it to the SS. No doubt he was afraid that he would be fired from his post or disciplined for failure to maintain order in his barrack.

At noon the next day, the authorities ordered us to go to the other end of C Camp. After we had stood in line for a while, they gave us each a tin mug, tin plate, spoon, and a ladle of soup from a 200-liter cauldron. It tasted so awful that I gave my serving to another inmate. Herman couldn't get it down, either.

Later in the day they led us to the administrative barrack and tattooed us on our left forearms with a pointed tool dipped in ink. I had a new identity. From now on I was A-8979. Herman was A-8980. An SS man gave a short speech, shrieking more than talking. We were concentration camp inmates, he told us. They would permit us to live as long as we could hold out. There was only one way out, and that was through the chimney. He finished up by saying, "*Ein Laus ist dein Todt*" (One louse will be your death).

Afterwards they lined us up along the main street of the camp to await new orders. Suddenly a huge group of teenaged boys came by, among them a friend of mine from Kolozsvar. I shouted his name, and when our eyes met, I asked him if he had seen Alexander, my younger brother. "Yes, he's here someplace," he said, "but I don't know where—there are 3,000 of us, you know."

The boys slowly vanished from sight in the direction of the gas chamber and crematorium. Smoke billowed continuously out of the chimney, and it reeked of burning flesh.

I had no chance of helping my little brother. Even if he had been able to break away from his group, he wouldn't have escaped his fate. Only by being tattooed like us could he have eluded death, at least for the time being. Nevertheless, the sight of those innocent children being herded to their death, as well as my powerlessness to save my little brother, has haunted me for more than sixty years.

While those of us who have been chosen to perform slave labor wait to leave Auschwitz-Birkenau, a group of thousands of boys passes right in front of us, their arms linked. They are of all different ages, but most of them seem to be teenagers.

"WORK WILL MAKE YOU FREE"

A LITTLE WHILE AFTER I saw my brother walk to his death arm-in-arm with thousands of other boys, those of us who had been chosen to perform slave labor started off for the labor camp. We each got a ration of bread at the gate, but few of us could eat it, although we were very hungry. It wasn't a long march. It was only a few miles to Auschwitz I, the main camp, which consisted of several two-story brick buildings. Above the entrance to the camp were the words that have now become notorious: *Arbeit macht frei* (Work will make you free).

The authorities led our group of approximately 1,000 inmates to the bath house. For several hours we just stood there waiting our turn, but the line hardly moved. Aware that the gas chambers were camouflaged as shower rooms, many of the inmates at the front of the line didn't dare to go inside. I grabbed Herman from the back of the line, and we went in together to shower. Our lives as slave laborers had begun.

Shortly afterwards leading German industrialists began to show up and select skilled inmates to work in their factories. Turners, carpenters, welders, and ironsmiths were the first inmates allowed to leave the camp. Since I had often helped my father during vacation time, I had put myself down as a watchmaker. My brother had registered as a goldsmith, the vocation for which he had been trained. But none of the industrialists seemed to be interested in either of those trades.

As we stood in formation one day, a privileged inmate—a so-called scribe—came up and began to write down our inmate numbers. After passing me by, he added Herman to his list. Since I was terror-stricken at the thought that my brother and I would be separated, I followed after the scribe and pleaded with him to add me to the list.

"No, that's out of the question," he said. "You're too weak for the work these people are going to do." I asked him what kind of work it was. After hesitating a little, he answered that it was in the coal mines. I told him that I could handle it, just as long as my brother and I could stay together. He tried to get me to be quiet, but I refused to give up. At last he got tired of arguing and asked me if I knew Herman's number. "Of course," I said. "A-8980." He found the number and crossed it off the list.

I've always thought that my stubbornness—not to mention my tears—saved Herman from a certain death. The coal mines were probably the most unbearable work sites of all; the older inmates told us that everyone who worked there soon broke down. A normal inmate could handle it for seven or eight weeks at the most. They gave each laborer only minimum rations and forced him to mine a certain amount of coal every day. The farther he fell behind in his quota during regular working hours, the longer he had to work at night to make up for it. It was a vicious cycle that soon made him totally unfit for work and a sure candidate for Birkenau's gas chamber.

One afternoon the word went out that they needed volunteers for the night shift in the kitchen. Only a few inmates had offered to work, and more were needed. I heard that they were looking for watchmakers. Hoping to be transferred to a more liveable camp, Herman and I volunteered immediately. But it was only a trick. They marched us straight to the kitchen and made us peel potatoes all night long.

Peeling and peeling, I tried to fight my sleepiness. Finally the chef came up and said that I could lie down for a while in his office. Thanking him for his kindness, I stretched out to rest. Soon he started to fuss about in such a strange way that it wasn't hard to figure out what he was after. But I acted innocent and naïve, and he finally gave up.

As luck would have it, they transferred us the next day to another camp, Buna-Monowitz, otherwise known as Auschwitz III. It was located a few miles east of the enormous I. G. Farben Works. The factory, which was under construction at the time, later produced gasoline and synthetic rubber.

At first we slept in a long, rectangular quarantine tent, where it was terribly hot. We had nothing to eat or drink and suffered horribly. A couple of days later we finally moved into Barrack 32.

The barrack captain was a German political prisoner. We figured that out from the color of the triangle sewn beside the inmate number on the breast of his jacket. The political prisoners usually treated us pretty decently, but this guy was an exception.

On our first day of work, we marched out through the gate of the Buna-Monowitz Camp and past the camp orchestra. Every time we went by this point on the way to or from work, we heard them playing. It was several miles to the site where Herman and I were to work as cement mixers. My job was to carry 110-pound sacks back and forth. It was very strenuous, but I was afraid to slow down. Finally, one of the older inmates whispered to me to rest a little between runs. But as soon as an SS officer came into view, I had to speed up again. If I didn't, he was likely to beat me.

Our only chance to rest was between 12:00 and 12:30, when they served us a disgusting concoction called Buna-soup, a watery green brew made from something that looked like blades of grass. It tasted disgusting. But we needed the liquid, since the water near the worksite was undrinkable.

At 5:00 we marched back to the camp. By that time, we were totally wiped out. We passed the camp orchestra, which was playing *Alte Kameraden*, a German march. Before going to our barracks, we had to line up for inspection, or "call." That could take up to a couple of hours if things didn't go our way.

When the inspection was over, they finally gave us our daily meal: one liter of soup, a quarter loaf of bread, a pat of margarine, and a slice of sausage (usually blood sausage) or a little piece of cheese. On Fridays they gave us a tablespoon of marmalade to put on our bread.

The barrack captain was in charge of handing out the food. He carefully checked our inmate numbers off his list in order to make sure that nobody got two servings. We always waited with baited breath to see how far he would dip his ladle into the cauldron. The further down it went, the thicker the soup. We ate everything right on the spot. It wasn't a good idea to try to save a piece of bread for morning, since another inmate would probably steal it in the meantime.

In the morning they served us a brownish liquid that they tried to pretend was coffee. Except for the Buna-soup at lunch, they didn't

There were several camp orchestras in Auschwitz. The orchestra in Buna-Monowitz had a permanent spot by the gate. It played every morning when we marched to work, and every evening when we returned. The tune was always the same: **Alte Kameraden**, *a German march.*

give us any more food until evening. Our hunger pangs were almost unbearable.

They awakened us every morning at 5:00 sharp. The barrack assistants pounded on the bedsteads with their clubs and shouted, "Up and at 'em, you lazy dogs!" Anyone who didn't immediately jump out of bed was in trouble. I could hardly move after the first day of work. Although I was stiff and aching all over, I had to shuffle to my feet, make my bed, and get ready to march—first to inspection and then to the cement works.

They had assigned Herman to another work team, Command 26, which had a real brute, a capo by the name of Hugo, as foreman. We soon discovered that the work drained our strength. If we continued at our original pace on our minimal food rations, we wouldn't survive more than a couple of months.

Since Herman could play the violin pretty well, he decided to try

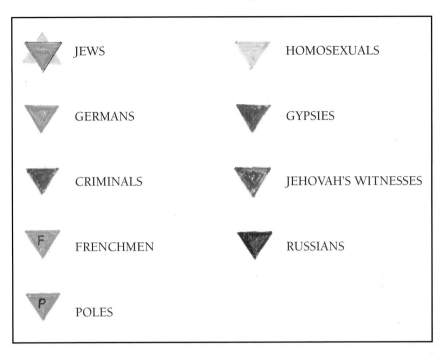

JEWS		HOMOSEXUALS	
GERMANS		GYPSIES	
CRIMINALS		JEHOVAH'S WITNESSES	
FRENCHMEN		RUSSIANS	
POLES			

The Germans used different symbols in order to distinguish between the various categories of prisoners within the camps.

to get into the camp orchestra. He asked the orchestra director one day if he could join them. The director handed him a violin and told him to play something. But since Herman was nervous and hadn't practiced for a while, he didn't play well enough for the director. The man kicked him out of the orchestra barrack and told him never to show his face there again.

So Herman had to work in Command 26. Hugo had a green triangle next to his inmate number, which meant that he was a criminal. There were rumors that he was serving a life sentence for murdering his wife. One day Herman gathered his courage and told Hugo that he had been trained as a goldsmith. If Herr Capo would be so kind as to give him a silver coin, Herman would gladly turn it into piece of jewelry. Hugo bawled him out for having gone directly to him—he should have asked the aide-de-camp first. But the very next day he gave Herman an old two-mark silver coin.

There was a little workshop for welding, forging, and carpentry.

The first day in the camp I couldn't bring myself to eat the soup they served us. It smelled and tasted disgusting. But after only a few weeks, I was willing to do almost anything to get something to eat. Here my friend Tibbi and I helped ourselves to the half-rotten contents of a garbage can that a Polish peasant was taking from the kitchen to feed to his hogs.

They let Herman work in a little corner of it. By evening he had finished a pair of earrings. Hugo was surprised and pleased by what Herman had been able to do under such primitive conditions. From then on Herman was one of the camp goldsmiths. Command 26 worked mostly at the central depot, an enormous building with rust-proof pipes of all sizes suitable for the forging of rings that the capo could sell.

I was assigned odd jobs here and there. One day I was with an older Hungarian friend named Tibor, Tibbi for short. He asked me to keep a lookout for a horse-drawn cart that came at the same time every week. When the cart came into view, he told me to take a bowl and follow him. Just as we walked up to the cart, the Polish peasant slowed down. On the back of the cart were two large wooden barrels containing garbage and left-over food that he was taking to feed his hogs. Without thinking twice, we dipped our bowls into the barrels. It felt like an eternity since that day I had turned up my nose at the soup on our first day at Auschwitz-Birkenau.

I had frequent dreams during my time in the camp. They were almost always nightmares, and of a very special kind. Of course, our daily life was a nightmare in itself. In my nocturnal dream world, I repeatedly tried to convince myself that the evil all around me was simply a nightmare from which I would soon awake. But each morning I awoke to the same painful realization that the nightmare was nothing less than reality itself.

The first hanging I witnessed was of the camp dentist. They claimed that his books didn't tally, that some of the gold fillings hadn't been entered. On the way to the gallows, the condemned man resisted. However, once the noose was around his neck, he kicked away the footstool even before the steel-helmeted military policeman had finished reading the death warrant.

IN THE SHADOW
OF THE GALLOWS

O
NE AFTERNOON WE were passing through the gate on the way back from work and the orchestra was playing its usual nerve-racking music. Suddenly I discovered to my horror that a gallows had been erected in the area where we had inspection twice a day. It was constructed from thick logs, painted black, and equipped with noose and trapdoor. The older prisoners gave a sigh of resignation. They knew this meant that our evening meal would be delayed for at least an hour.

While roll was being called, an inmate came along with an SS officer on either side of him. When he saw the gallows, he stopped short and refused to go any further. The SS officers had to drag him the last thirty steps. As he stood on the footstool, he tried desperately to turn his head away from the executioner, who was struggling to slip the noose around his neck. But after one of the camp's most feared SS officers walked up and said something to him, he seemed to give up.

As soon as the noose was fastened, the steel-helmeted military policeman began to read the death warrant. But before he could finish reading, the inmate—in a desperate protest, and clearly upsetting the SS officer—kicked away the footstool he was standing on.

After the inmate had hung there for fifteen minutes, we filed past him, barrack by barrack. We found out later that he had been the camp dentist. During a raid on his office, they had discovered that some gold fillings hadn't been entered in his books. At Auschwitz that was all they needed to condemn him to death.

There were quite a few English prisoners of war working in the factory. They were always neatly dressed, their jackets and trousers well-pressed; they didn't seem to have much to complain about. One day when I was working at the power station, I got into a conversation with one of them. He asked why I was there. When I answered that it was because I was Jewish, he got red as a beet, began to swear at me, and blurted out the grossest imaginable anti-Semitic insults.

It was particularly painful to hear such obscenities from a soldier who was fighting against Nazi Germany. Physical abuse would have been much easier to put up with.

There were many Polish civilian laborers who had a similar attitude to us Jews, but they didn't show their hatred as much as the British prisoner. Though they occasionally let a taunt slip out, the worst thing was to see the contempt in their eyes

About a week after the hanging, we had to witness a second one. This time we stood only twenty to twenty-five yards from the execution site. A young man was led up to the gallows.

After they read the death warrant, the trap door fell. But something had gone haywire, and after more than fifteen minutes, he was still hanging there alive. Nobody made a sound. The boy continued to thrash his legs in panic, and the only thing we heard was the creaking of the gallows.

Finally even the executioners had seen enough. The camp capo, a powerfully built guy, went up to the gallows, grabbed the boy's feet and tugged on them as hard as he could in order to get the noose to tighten. Still it took an unbearably long time for the boy to die.

A young Frenchman standing next to me muttered *merde allemands* (goddamned Germans)! The sixteen-year-old boy had been his best friend.

One person I'll never forget was our barrack captain, a German political prisoner. He seemed to enjoy seeing us suffer. More than once he showed that he didn't like how we had made our beds by ordering us to stand for several minutes with our knees bent. That was very hard on us, especially after a full day's work. He raised his club and beat the inmates who gave up and squatted down.

Looking back, I've thought a lot about the reason for his sadistic outbursts. It might have had to do with the fact that our barrack was located right next to the camp brothel. Polish women were forced to work there. The camp management went there regularly, but our barrack captain had apparently been banned from the premises. It is quite possible that he tortured us because of his resentment.

The second hanging I had to witness was especially cruel. The noose snarled around the neck of the sixteen-year-old boy, and he was still alive after struggling for fifteen minutes. In order to put an end to the whole thing, a capo went up to the gallows and tugged on his legs.

Despite the fact that the camp capo pulled as hard as he could, it was another few minutes until the boy finally died.

Our barrack captain leads us in punishment drills after a strenuous day's work. He physically abused the inmates who couldn't remain in the agonizing position. The excuse he gave for the drills was that he wasn't satisfied with how we had made our beds.

For us ordinary inmates hunger for food took the place of lust for women. My fondest wish was to stuff myself on white bread heaped with margarine and marmalade.

Herman, who was now an official goldsmith and privileged inmate, finally managed to get me into Command 26. He told the capo that I was good at drawing and graphics. They assigned me to the depot office, where I kept inventory of the welding tubes and designed greeting cards. Since the factory was located in Poland, there were no cards available in German. That meant that the capo had a ready market among German civilians and privileged inmates. Now I didn't have to do so much backbreaking labor. And I occasionally got a little extra something to eat.

At lunch one day an especially cruel SS officer caught a Jewish inmate accepting a bowl of soup from a Polish civilian. The soup they gave the Polish civilians was much more edible than what we inmates got. Just as the inmate was starting to eat, the SS officer asked sarcastically if he would like some more extra rations. After ordering him to bend over, he looked around for a weapon. At last he found a shovel shaft.

He began to strike the poor inmate as hard as he could; after only a few blows, the man lost consciousness. However, the SS officer continued the beating until the wooden handle fell off. But he still hadn't had enough. Finding a second shovel, he resumed the beating, despite the fact that the inmate seemed to be lifeless. The rest of us had to watch the whole thing. I was terror-stricken that he would find some reason to abuse me as well. But finally he got tired of it, threw down the shovel shaft next to the motionless body, and went off. One of the inmates in our group, a doctor, examined the bleeding man and announced that he was dead.

One of the cruelest SS officers in the Auschwitz II camp beats a Polish Jew to death with a shovel. The inmate's only crime is that he has accepted a bowl of soup from a civilian laborer.

Allied planes had bombed Auschwitz. One of the inmates returned from work with both legs blown off. Amazingly, he was still conscious. He sat straight up on a door that four other inmates were carrying in through the gates of Auschwitz III.

THE FIRST BOMBS

THE FIRST ALLIED air raids on Auschwitz that I experienced were on August 20, 1944, a bright sunshiny Sunday. Normally we worked every other Sunday, and this was my day off. The howl of air-raid sirens was nothing new for us, but this time it was for real—we could hear the bombs exploding. When a bomb fell right in the middle of the camp, I ran into the barrack and crawled under my bed, hoping to protect myself from flying splinters.

Half an hour later they sounded the all-clear signal. I glanced over at the factory and saw enormous clouds of black smoke billowing out. At first, I felt elated; the Nazis had finally taken a good beating. But then I realized that Herman was working in the factory. Feeling terrified, I sneaked as close to the gate as I dared. Since the area was swarming with SS officers—who weren't likely to be in the best of moods just now—it wasn't a very good idea to get too close.

Eventually the other inmates returned from work. The first thing I saw coming through the gate was a group of four inmates carrying a wooden door on their shoulders. On top of the door sat another inmate, both of whose legs had been blown away. Amazingly, he seemed to be fully conscious. But there was terror in his eyes. He surely realized that a legless inmate would quickly be sent to the gas chamber.

When I finally saw Herman limping into the camp, I felt as if a big weight had been lifted from my chest. He told me that he had jumped into a big steel pipe in the depot yard when the first bomb exploded. Only a few moments later, a 500-pound bomb had struck down right near him. The air pressure from the explosion had caused the pipe to fly into the air. He bruised his hip when the pipe landed a dozen yards away, but otherwise he was uninjured.

The factory was bombed more and more often. Our lives were constantly in danger. Of course, they didn't allow inmates into the air-raid shelters. The shelters were reserved for civilians and guards. We had to rely on our own resourcefulness to avoid the bombs.

The safest place was the east end of the factory, behind a huge coal deposit. But we didn't always have time to run that far. Instead, we would fall to the ground, cover our heads, and hope that no bomb would explode too close to us. One day the bombs started to go off when I was still a long way from the coal deposit. The earth trembled under my feet. When I looked up, I saw a bomb coming straight at me.

I don't think I've ever been so afraid in my whole life, either before or after. By some miracle the bomb missed me by some fifty yards.

Splinters from anti-aircraft grenades were also dangerous. The sharp, hot shards of metal rained down all over the place. We shielded our heads with tin plates. We envied the crews that flew high above us. In a few hours they would be returning to the freedom and security of their bases.

UNDER THE YOKE
OF THE MASTER RACE

A S I MENTIONED earlier, the only personal possessions they allowed us to keep when we entered Auschwitz were our shoes and waist belts. Shoes soon became a life-and-death matter. If an inmate's own shoes were in poor condition, he had to order a pair of wooden camp shoes with canvas uppers. They were heavy, awkward, and rubbed badly—and that could lead to serious wounds. Because of our poor diet, the wounds healed slowly. For inmates with wooden shoes, the long daily marches to and from work were a major ordeal.

Fortunately, both Herman and I had brought good shoes with us, but eventually even they began to wear out. After making some secret contacts, Herman finally managed to get his hands on a slab of synthetic rubber, enough to resole our shoes. The only problem was how to get the rubber into the camp and to a shoemaker. Once we had done that, we could pay the shoemaker with bread or cigarettes, which were the camp's hard currency.

Smuggling in the rubber was more dangerous than you might think. The *Rapportführer,* an SS non-commissioned officer assigned to count the number of inmates passing through the gate each morning and evening, was an expert at picking out inmates at random and performing body searches. Anyone caught with something unauthorized in his possession was in serious trouble. The culprit was locked into the narrow area between the two electric barbed-wire fences. There he would wait for his punishment, which could be anything from twenty-five lashes to death.

Even the lashes themselves could be deadly. It all depended on who meted them out and what wounds he caused. If the wounds were slow to heal and the inmate could no longer work as hard as before, he could end up in the gas chamber.

I decided to take my chances and try to smuggle the rubber slab into the camp. Fortunately, the *Rapportführer* didn't search me as I came through the gate. Since Herman had received cigarettes for some jewelry he had made, we could afford to have our shoes re-soled. Neither of us smoked, and that increased our chances of survival. Smokers often traded away their meager bread rations for a cigarette.

One day I glanced up while making an enlargement from a lithograph of a famous German painting. An SS officer was standing there looking over my shoulder. Since it was against the rules to do such things during working hours, I was scared out of my wits. But luck was on my side.

He stared for a while at the half-completed enlargement and then asked whether I could do a portrait of him. Though portraiture wasn't my strong point, I had no choice but to say that I would try.

Since he didn't have time to sit as a model, he gave me a little passport photo taken many years earlier. I tried to memorize his now-wrinkled face and hope that he would be satisfied with what I could accomplish. I was relieved that he didn't have time to pose as a model. His terrifying presence would have made it impossible for me to complete a portrait that he would have found satisfactory.

Fortunately he was quite pleased. He even asked which barrack I was in, so that he could order the captain to give me some extra rations. That never happened, of course, but I was just glad that I had gotten away without being punished.

To escape blows, whippings, and other kinds of assault was a rare, almost absurd quirk of fate. Many camp authorities took every chance they could get to show off their feelings of supremacy and their master-race mentality. One time, I was ordered to walk around the depot yard and write down the serial numbers of some newly-arrived, fully-loaded welding tubes. A German foreman, wearing the badge of the Nazi Party on the lapel of his coat, was helping me. Suddenly a pretty, young Russian woman in civilian clothes came by.

[OPPOSITE]: *Fortunately, I didn't have to do manual labor in the factory at Buna-Monowitz. Instead they assign me to do office work and design German greeting cards. They also order me to do portraits. I did one of an SS officer, who had left me his passport photo to work from.*

Scenting prey, he lost all interest in our work, called her over, and told her to follow him to a little building nearby. In the most unmistakable way possible, he demonstrated with his fingers what he was planning to do to her.

"Please, I can't," she said in a trembling voice. "I'm a virgin."

"In that case I'm sure we can arrange it so that you come to a concentration camp and there you will wear a striped uniform like this man here," he said, pointing at me. Dragging her into the building, he closed the door behind them.

One day the most feared of all the SS officers walked into the little workshop where Herman worked along with five or six other craftsmen. It was the same officer who had brutally killed an inmate several days earlier for accepting someone else's soup. He asked in a loud voice, "Who's the goldsmith here?" Trembling with fright, Herman had to admit that he was the goldsmith.

After walking up to Herman's work table, the officer took a handful of gold fillings out of his pocket and explained that he wanted him to make a ring with the SS emblem welded on top. That was quite a complicated task and required real goldsmith's tools. But the camp didn't have those kinds of tools. However, Herman had to accept the job. The officer asked when he could pick up the ring. Herman answered that he could have it by Friday, four days later. Giving him an icy look, the officer took out his pistol and pointed it at his temple. "What day did you say?" Herman answered in a trembling voice, "Wednesday, sir." Tensing his finger on the trigger, the officer said, "I need the ring tomorrow morning. What do you say now?"

Herman realized that the officer wouldn't think twice about pulling the trigger, especially if he kept repeating that it would take a couple of days. Finally, he mumbled that he would try to finish it the very next day. "I'll be back tomorrow, and if you know what's good for you, you'll be done by then," said the officer as he strolled casually out of the workshop.

All the other craftsmen breathed a deep sigh of relief. For Herman it was a matter of do or die, and he finished the ring the next afternoon. Without thanking him, the officer went off with the ring on his finger. Most likely it had been made out of the same gold for which the dentist had been put to death.

A brutal SS officer walks up to Herman's work table. Taking a handful of gold fillings out of his pocket, he explains that he wants a ring with the SS emblem welded on top. With his pistol pointed at Herman's forehead, he makes it clear that he expects the ring to be done the following day.

On one of my Sundays off, a teenaged friend and I sat on the radiator that ran along one wall of the barrack and chatted. Suddenly a shot went off. My friend screamed and grabbed his left forearm. Blood had begun to ooze out and stain his shirt.

Several seconds of confusion went by before we realized that someone in the watchtower was having fun by firing into our barrack. The bullet had entered my friend's arm. We had no idea why the sentry had done it. Most likely he was bored and just wanted to mess around with us a little. We were fair game, of course.

Fortunately for my friend, the bullet had only caused a flesh wound, which healed without any serious complications. He didn't have to stay at the hospital for very long.

Going to the Revier Hospital was like playing Russian roulette. If an inmate was lucky, he got better quickly and was released. But the hospital administration could decide at any time to get rid of a patient by sending him to the Birkenau gas chamber.

The inmates who had been at the camp the longest said that it was like a rest home compared to the way it had been back in 1942–43. At that time the SS officers had been like rabid dogs. Nobody had been exempt from their bloodthirstiness. It had gotten to the point that the factory administration requested that camp commanders mete out the punishments inside the camp itself whenever possible. The brutal assaults were demoralizing for the civilian personnel.

When I came down with strep throat and a dangerously high fever, the old-timers strongly advised me not to go to the hospital. I continued to work as long as I could. But I had shivers and could barely make it to and from work.

Finally I could hardly stand up any longer and had to drag myself to the hospital.

I was lucky again. The doctor came from my hometown and did all he could to cure me. After a little more than a week I felt somewhat better and returned to work immediately. I didn't even consider remaining at the hospital long enough to fully recover. The smart thing was not to stay there a day longer than absolutely necessary.

I found out long afterwards that the strep throat had led to rheumatic fever, and that my recurrent joint problems were a direct result of that illness.

In October 1944 rumors began to circulate that it would soon be time for the feared elimination procedure. A group of SS doctors arrived from Birkenau and spread out through the barracks. All inmates, except for the privileged ones, had to take off their shirts and pass before one of these messengers of death. With a quick glance, the doctor would determine whether the inmate was worn down and ready to be discarded, or whether he was still usable in the work force.

[OPPOSITE]: *A document from my time at the Auschwitz III labor camp: a page from the camp hospital's register.*

A-8979 was the inmate number tattooed on my arm. I was admitted to the hospital on June 17, 1944, and discharged on June 26. The handwritten note "nach Birkenau" (to Birkenau) next to a prisoner's name indicated that he was no longer useful as a laborer and was being sent to the gas chamber. "Entlassen" meant that the prisoner had been discharged.

N - 10186   473

lfd. Nr.	Häftl. Nr.	Name	Zugang	Abgang	Bemerkungen
1370	173345	Roubiczer, Benjamin Jr.	17.6.44	1.7.44	Entlassen
1371	172658	Cohen, Prosper Jr.	"	26.6.44	Entlassen
1372	110658	de Voot, Joseph Jr.	"	4.6.44	Entlassen
1373	157977	Zero, Witold	"	20.6.44	Entlassen
1374	162741	Spolkowski, Stanislav	"	21.6.44	Entlassen
1375	A 3372	Volf, Fené Jr.	"	4.7.44	Entlassen
1376	162327	Dobrzynski, Israel	"	15.7.44	Entlassen
1377	194186	Cicierski, Antoni	"	20.6.44	Entlassen
1378	A 7157	Eisner, Nathan Jr.	"	21.6.44	Entlassen
1379	169874	Levy, Albert Jr.	"	20.6.44	Entlassen
1380	A 7718	Rosenfeld, Zoltan Jr.	"	21.6.44	Entlassen
1381	79789	Koprak, Smul Jr.	"	17.6.44	Entlassen
1382	145724	Urbaniak, Josef	"	"	Entlassen
1383	157949	van der Heide, Gered Jr.	"	20.6.44	Entlassen
1384	A 8979	Grünfeld, Benjamin Jr.	"	26.6.44	Entlassen
1385	175523	Silberschmidt, Ernst Jr.	"	1.7.44	Entlassen
1386	175302	Groenteman, Juda Jr.	"	22.6.44	Entlassen
1387	105041	Steinitz, Kurt Jr.	"	21.6.44	Entlassen
1388	A 6773	Feder, Andor Jr.	"	22.6.44	nach Sulmen
1389	116628	Blumenthal, Heinz Werner Jr.	"	26.6.44	Entlassen
1390	167531	Goldbum, Fankiel Jr.	"	"	Entlassen
1391	A 6788	Halpert, Sandor Jr.	"	21.6.44	Entlassen
1392	173367	Segal, Fankiel Jr.	"	17.6.44	nach Sulmen
1393	169763	Berger, Henri Jr.	"	19.7.44	Entlassen
1394	172382	Achwasser, Georg Jr.	"	22.6.44	Entlassen
1395	106978	Krenk, Hermann Jr.	"	29.6.44	Entlassen
1396	A 5822	Kate, David Jr.	"	26.6.44	Entlassen
1397	143993	Drucker, Siegfried Jr.	"	14.6.44	Entlassen
1398	60357	Luger, Josef	"	22.6.44	nach Sulmen
1399	139363	Slominski, Paul	"	1.7.44	Entlassen
1400	186995	Sonnenwald, Josef Jr.	18.6.44	3.7.44	Entlassen
1401	120640	Jakubik, Josef	"	21.6.44	Entlassen
1402	171963	Naarden, Michel Jr.	"	3.7.44	Entlassen

October 1944. Going from barrack to barrack, an SS doctor performs the routine elimination procedure that we inmates dread. Inmates who are too scrawny or too far gone in some other way are sent to Birkenau to be gassed and cremated.

The doctor points to me, indicating that I will be sent to the gas chamber. But at the last minute Hugo, my capo, convinces him to cross me off the list and my life is saved.

When it was my turn to stand before the doctor, he ordered his assistant to write down my number. He made the decision without hesitating for a moment. I was used up, no longer serviceable. But just then a miracle happened. Hugo, the capo for my work unit, walked in and asked the doctor to spare me. "This inmate is very useful to me, and I would like to keep him," he said. Obviously surprised, the doctor looked at him with raised eyebrows. It was rare that a capo tried to protect an inmate. But after hesitating a little, the doctor motioned to his assistant to cross my number off the list.

Thanks to Hugo I survived that elimination round. He came to the barrack just to rescue me. He knew that I was emaciated and in the danger zone.

Out of 12,000 inmates, a total of 2,000 were selected for elimination that day. As a kind of "going-away present," they each got an extra liter of soup before leaving for Birkenau's gas chamber.

Though more than sixty years have passed since the day I was almost chosen to be gassed and cremated, I still remember holding my little prayer book and thanking my Creator for having rescued me from death. Only a week earlier I had attended a secret Jewish New Year service in a remote corner of the camp.

The key to survival at Auschwitz was adaptability. Above all, you had to avoid drawing attention to yourself. If someone in a top position noticed you, the consequences were almost always fateful. If you got in the way of an SS officer when he was in a bad mood, your life was in danger. If you had the misfortune of running into an SS officer, you had to lift your cap. If you forgot to do it, he would normally subject you to serious physical abuse, which could lead to death. You definitely could not afford the luxury of self-pity. If you couldn't endure the dreary life without grumbling, you were asking for it. And if you looked resigned or angry or defiant, you were in even worse trouble. SS officers and the more brutal capos took that as a cue to beat you up. And in most cases they didn't stop until you were dead.

CHRISTMAS AND NEW YEAR

NEW PRISONERS ARRIVED at the camp all the time. When one of them brought a toilette bag with shaving equipment and soap to the lavatory one morning, I could hardly believe my eyes. He turned out to be a Dane who had been transferred from Theresienstadt. It was unheard of that he had been allowed to keep some of his personal belongings. It seemed like a very positive sign.

Several residents of the Lodz ghetto also came. Usually they were people who had enjoyed some kind of special status or held a high post in the ghetto. One of them was a very fine artist. His name, if my memory serves me right, was Hirsch Schülitz. He was assigned to work near me and devoted most of his time to portraiture. After looking at a person only once, he could do a portrait from memory.

Our *Bauleiter* (the boss at the central depot) was a Nazi bigwig who never gave me or my fellow inmates any trouble. When he found out about the skilled portrait artist, he brought him photographs of his wife and children and ordered a picture done of the whole family. The artist succeeded way beyond the *Bauleiter*'s expectations. As a reward, the *Bauleiter* gave him some pastries, which he shared with the rest of us.

A Belgian Jew in our group specialized in designing greeting cards, just as I did. Now that Christmas was approaching, the orders poured in. Herman's specialty was making jewelry—which was popular as a Christmas present—so his days were just as busy as ours.

Hugo, our capo, along with some other VIP's in our work command, had long since figured out how to take advantage of the craftsmen among the inmates. For example, he assigned a carpenter in our group to make a secret chamber for him on the upper level of the barrack. He needed someplace to take Polish civilian women. The carpenter constructed a little annex staircase that was impossible for an outsider to detect. Hugo was very pleased and gave him some cigarettes.

When Hugo began to limp after one of the air raids, the privileged inmates began to kid him. They asked him how he could get a thigh injury from the bomb splinters without his trousers being torn. He had been in his secret chamber during the raid. We never passed up a chance to joke around. Laughter was a safety valve.

One day a foreman, a Hamburg Jew named Julius, told me to go to one of the camp tailors and get my measurements taken. I was going to get a customized uniform like the ones nearly all the privileged prisoners wore. In my new clothing, I was basically exempt from the worst abuse, at least as long as I didn't slip up too badly.

In order to improve our work performance, the authorities brought a dozen or so women inmates to the camp for us to have sex with. But not many of the ordinary prisoners took advantage of the opportunity. Just like us, the women were human wrecks at this point. We used whatever drive we still had left in order to survive.

Around this time the factory administration introduced something called the *Prämienschein*, a kind of bonus premium for especially hard workers. Inmates could use the premiums to buy either toothpaste or *Machorka*, a crumbly tobacco-like substance. One day an SS officer gave Herman some premiums for some jewelry he had made. The officer told him reassuringly that the war would soon be over. That was like a shot of vitamins for us. Every SS officer wasn't a monster after all. The war wouldn't last forever. Things like that gave us hope that we just might survive the war.

Some of the most talented inmates gave a New Year's Eve show. Since Herman and I had tailor-made uniforms, the authorities let us in. The room was packed with SS personnel and privileged inmates. In one act that I remember very clearly, an inmate did some quick sketches, none of which seemed to be of anything in particular. But when he turned them upside down, the pictures suddenly appeared. For a while we forgot all about the dismal life at the camp. It soothed our aching souls. The evening reminded us of how important it was to have a little entertainment once in a while.

After New Year, the authorities ordered us to carry two bricks from the factory to the outskirts of the camp every day. Within a couple of days, the pile was already quite high. We suspected that we were contributing to our own deaths, that the bricks would be used to build a new crematorium and gas chamber.

Not many of us really believed at the beginning of 1945 that we had a chance to survive; we knew too much about the terrible things that had happened at Auschwitz. The last inmates who arrived at our camp had all held high positions at Auschwitz-Birkenau. They gave us the awful details of the mass killings, so we had a pretty good idea of how extensive they were.

We were sure that the Nazis considered us to be witnesses to their atrocities. So they would make sure to silence us once and for all, just as they had already silenced millions of other people.

On Thursday, January 18, 1945, after a long day of work, we have to march westward instead of getting the evening soup we look forward to so much. It is an insane, nightmarish march without food, drink, or sleep. Inmates who can't go any further are shot on the spot. The bodies of dead inmates litter the side of the road. We don't arrive at the Polish city of Gleiwitz until late Saturday night.

WE MARCH WESTWARD

IN THE MIDDLE of January 1945, the reinforced Russian army advanced westward. After work on January 18, when all we wanted to do was return to the camp for a badly needed meal and rest, we had to stand at the inspection area for several hours. Finally everyone in the camp, except for the sick inmates, began to march westward.

After only a couple of hours we were worn out, hungry and sleepy. By this time we were used to hunger and thirst, but being deprived of sleep was a new and painful experience. Herman had an extra burden to bear—literally. An armed guard ordered him to carry his backpack.

Herman and I took turns carrying the backbreaking load, but finally our strength was about to give out. We realized that we would never make it the whole way carrying the pack, but we couldn't figure out how to get rid of it. Finally we just mixed in with the long line of staggering inmates and put the backpack down in the snow at the side of the road. We never saw the guard again.

In order to keep going on the slushy road, we made an agreement with our Hungarian friend Tibor that the three of us would stay together. Each of us would walk in the middle for a few minutes at a time with his arms draped around the shoulders of the other two. That way we could all get a little sleep without falling behind. We did that all of Thursday night and Friday. On Saturday afternoon we finally stopped for a couple of hours at a deserted factory area. We all huddled together in cold sheds and fell asleep.

When the guards prodded us up and ordered us to go on, it had started to get dark. We felt as though we had slept for only a few minutes. One of the guards knocked off the butt of his rifle trying to beat some life into a few of the inmates. Whenever we heard a rifle go off, we knew that someone hadn't been able to march any further. Sometimes the guards shot inmates who had merely staggered out of line.

[55]

Late Saturday night we arrived at the outskirts of the city of Gleiwitz, where there was an evacuated camp. When Herman came up to the gate, he stopped short and refused to go on. His eyes were wide open and frightened.

When I asked him what the matter was, he said in a trembling voice that we would be killed in this camp; he could feel it in his bones. I explained to him that we had to follow the others inside. But he just stood there rooted to the spot and repeated that we were going to be killed. I kept telling him that the guards would soon notice us and shoot us right away, but I couldn't talk any sense into him.

At last I realized that he had had a nervous breakdown. The trick was to act fast. Realizing that only a shock could pull him out of it, I gave him two hard slaps, one after the other. That broke his obsessive train of thought, and he followed me into the camp without resistance. It was the first and last time I ever hit my brother.

Much later I realized that he had been worried mostly about me. Of course, he was suffering from exhaustion, hunger, and thirst, just like the rest of us. But he was also weighed down by the responsibilities of a big brother. He was terrified that the hardships would be too much for me and that I would give up. And I'm certain that if Herman and Tibor hadn't been there to support me, I would never have survived the terrible march from Auschwitz.

The evacuated camp had been built for something like 5,000 inmates. The group that tried to squeeze into the wooden barracks consisted of at least twice that number. Soon I was the one who was panic-stricken. I felt as if I were about to suffocate, and I half-screamed at Herman, "We've got to get out of here." Somehow we managed to elbow our way out of the barrack. We walked around trying to find another barrack, but they were all packed. The only area that wasn't overflowing with exhausted inmates was the lavatory. Unfortunately, it had tin sides that left gaps of several inches at the floor and roof. But we climbed into the wash basin and fell asleep right away, clinging tightly to each other.

The next morning we saw the horrible results of the overcrowding. In each barrack there were twenty to thirty inmates who had been crushed to death.

In the afternoon it was time for inspection and check-off. An hour lat-

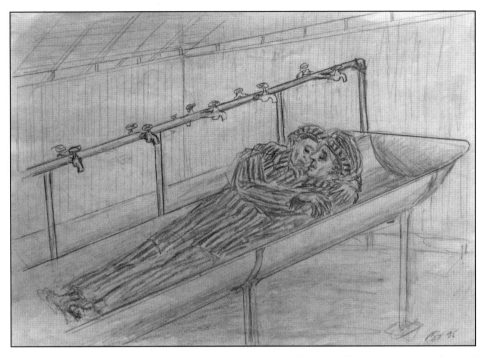

At Gleiwitz 10,000 of us squeeze into barracks that were intended for only half as many inmates. It feels as if I am about to suffocate, and I am panic-stricken. Herman and I manage to make our way out of the barrack and into the cold night. The only sheltered area that isn't overflowing with inmates is the lavatory. We lie down in the long wash basin and fall asleep right away.

er they ordered us to a second inspection. When an inmate in our group said, "Goddamn it anyway, they just counted us," an SS officer charged at him like a wild bull and beat him until he was bleeding all over.

A while later we had to pass by a group of SS officers, who divided the long column into two groups.

They directed inmates to the right or left on a purely random basis. Herman and I dashed to the right without waiting for the SS officer to give us a sign. Apparently he was in a hurry to complete the process, because he didn't say anything. Shortly afterwards the inmates in the left group marched out of the camp. We found out later that they had gone to Buchenwald and that very few of them had survived the war.

Those of us in the other group stayed at the camp until the following night, when they ordered us out of bed. Each of us received an inch-thick slice of sausage that was heavily salted and made us very thirsty. But before we had time to drink anything, they herded us out and made us run between SS guards, who were swinging their rifles wildly. Outside the camp was a train of flatcars; the inmates gradually filled them to the brim. It was so crowded that everyone except the privileged inmates had to stand up. When the train was completely full, the authorities shot the rest of the inmates.

Herman and I were lucky once again. Since we were among the first to climb on board, we wound up in a corner of the flatcar. Three privileged prisoners and their lackeys had claimed the corner for themselves, and anyone who crowded in on them was in trouble. If an inmate even staggered in their direction, he was immediately met with a flurry of blows from their clubs. Nevertheless, their cruelty offered Herman and me a little protection.

After what must have been five days, more than thirty prisoners lay dead in our flatcar. I could never have dreamed that I would ever have wanted to return to the Buna-Monowitz camp—at the camp we had at least had a daily ration of food and a bed to sleep in.

When we pulled into a dead end at one of the stations, the SS officers shouted for volunteers to carry off the corpses. At that point we were all half-crazed from hunger and thirst, so Herman volunteered, hoping to find something to drink. The dead bodies were simply flung onto the track and then carried away to be piled up on the other side of the platform. Passing by the steam engine, Herman asked the engineer for a little water. The engineer gave him a bowlful, which he immediately gulped down. Herman even got a refill, so that I could drink too. But after I had taken a couple of swallows, a group of inmates jumped on me and tore the bowl out of my hands. During the brawl that followed, all the water spilled out and we all tried to lick up the drops from our clothing.

The journey continued for five more days. By the time it was over, half of the inmates were dead or dying. Our friend Tibor, who had helped us survive the march, whispered one day that he had given up and couldn't hold out any longer. The next morning he was dead. Those were horrible days.

I thought that I was next in line to die. I began to search my heart, bitterly regretting that I wouldn't have the chance to repent for my

In the middle of the night the camp authorities herd us from the overcrowded camp at Gleiwitz to the depot, where a train is waiting for us. They force us to run between SS guards, who strike out at us as we crawl onto the flatcars.

sins by helping my relatives and fellow human beings. I realized that I had fought with my younger brother and disobeyed my parents too often. My whole life passed before my eyes, and there wasn't much there that I could really be proud of.

Late at night nine days after we had left the camp, we arrived at what we thought was our final destination. The train stopped outside a concentration camp that was all lit up. But the authorities said that the camp was full and that we would have to go on. The next day we came to a new camp. Finally they let us get out. Only those who could walk without help were allowed into the camp. The rest were shot. Somehow I managed to stagger into the camp. You have to remember that I had just sat unmoving for ten days under hellish conditions. The worst thing about the journey had been the thirst— it had almost driven us out of our minds. I can still remember seeing one of the inmates drinking his own urine out of a jar.

I have thought a lot about what enabled us to survive the ten-day train journey after our evacuation from Auschwitz. In addition, we had gone without food for four days before leaving, except for one heavily-salted piece of sausage. Nor did we get anything to eat the whole first day at Dora. Herman got hold of just water on the fifth day, and I also took a few swallows. That was certainly essential to our survival. Also, we lay completely still for ten days in the cold freight car; that reduced our energy consumption to a minimum.

The motto *Carpe diem* (seize the day) took on a very special significance in the camps. I began to realize that the phrase means not only seizing the day for yourself, but also helping your fellow man before it is too late. I was very close to dying of cold, thirst, and hunger during the ten-day train journey from Gleiwitz to Dora-Mittelbau, but I was not really afraid of dying. What I was afraid of was dying before I had accomplished something useful; and that thought upset me to no end.

Only the hardiest inmates survived more than a year in the camps. It was a miracle that both Herman and I held out. Most of the prisoners were sent to the gas chamber during the first or second quarterly elimination rounds. It was an even greater miracle that I came out alive after three death sentences. If we had given up, we would have been sent to the gas chamber. But we kept up the struggle, and that was the key to our survival. It may not be possible for someone who wasn't there to understand that death was always on our minds. The artfully hard-boiled cruelty of the Germans made death so degrading that it gave us strength to carry on the fight.

[OPPOSITE]: *The midwinter journey from Gleiwitz in flatcars takes ten days. When the train finally stops at Dora-Mittelbau, half of the passengers are dead.*

DORA-MITTELBAU

THE CAMP WE had come to was called Dora-Mittelbau. It was at the foot of a mountain and surrounded by spruce and pine woods. The barracks dotted the mountainside. It was a lovely panorama—if you can speak of a concentration camp as lovely.

It was a steep climb to the bath house, but we were so thirsty that nothing could have stopped us. When we got there, they ordered us to get undressed outside in the February cold. It seemed like an eternity before it was my turn to go in. I'll never again enjoy a shower as much as I did that one—though you really couldn't call it a shower in the normal sense of the word. I stood there with my mouth wide open and let the warm water stream down my throat.

While we were still naked, they led us to a large building. We had to wait there twenty-four hours before they gave us fresh uniforms. Finally I could read from the little prayer book I had still managed to hold onto. I thanked the Lord for giving me the strength to survive the journey. I really don't think I could have held out another day.

When I glanced at myself in a mirror several days later, I was totally shocked. I didn't recognize the face that stared back. I looked more like a skeleton than the young boy who had left Kolozsvar nine months earlier.

Maybe we were at a new camp, but the war went on just as always. The loudspeakers in the barracks blared out victory bulletins about the latest German offensive in the Ardenner Forest. However, after a few weeks the war began to go against the Germans and the loudspeakers fell silent.

Dora-Mittelbau was a labor camp. Nearly all of the inmates worked

[OPPOSITE]: *When we get to the Dora-Mittelbau labor camp, the authorities order us into the bath house. I have been in an open flatcar surrounded by dead and dying people for ten days, and the shower is an unbelievable luxury for me. I stand there with my mouth wide open and let the warm water stream down my throat.*

in the Nordhausen arms factory, which was dug into the mountain in two large connecting tunnels. In one tunnel the V1 rocket, the so-called flying bomb, was manufactured. The V2 rocket, which was so big that two freight cars were needed to carry it from the factory, was produced in the second tunnel. Outside the tunnels a large stock of rocket parts was hidden under camouflage nets.

Herman was assigned to a work command, which had its own barrack. I wound up in a different barrack, where half of the inmates were Italian prisoners of war. Our strapping barrack captain had been a Czech politician. I could tell right off that he was an educated man. Since Romanian, which I could speak pretty well, is related to Italian, the Italians could understand me. They received Red Cross packages on a regular basis and let me share a little of their food. Herman visited me in the evenings, and sometimes I managed to save a little soup for him.

Herman was emaciated at this point, a mere shadow of his former self. Dressed in a woman's ugly black coat with his inmate number on the chest, he would sit next to me and lick his spoon and bowl over and over again. Both Herman and I easily fit into the category of the most emaciated inmates.

An asphalt road behind our barrack led to the crematorium. One day a large semi-trailer truck came down the road and stopped in front of us. The driver got out and walked down to the crematorium. When he returned fifteen minutes later, he undid the tarpaulin in back and let down the flap. I could see right into the cargo area, but it took me a few seconds to realize what was inside. The trailer was filled with naked corpses.

A group of inmates came from the crematorium area pushing a rubber-tired cart, and the macabre unloading process began. Since the bodies weren't particularly skinny, it was obvious that these inmates hadn't died of hunger.

A good friend of Herman lay seriously ill in one of the barracks. His name was Bandi Markowitz and he was a skilled boxer. When we visited him one evening, he whispered to us that he had done a lot of boxing for the entertainment of SS officers and privileged inmates. He had come down with pneumonia and realized that he had no chance of recovering. He wanted us to take the food that he had left untouched by the side of the bed. Although we were very hungry, we couldn't bring ourselves to take it. We tried to console him by saying that his strong constitution would pull him through. But the next time we visited him, his bed was empty.

I had had a crush on a classmate named Ilona. Now her father was an inmate at the camp. He asked me to give his love to his daughter and other family members if I ever ran into them. He knew that he couldn't hold out much longer. He died shortly afterwards, thinking about his family to the very last. To my great regret, I haven't been able to carry out his final wish. I've never run across a single member of his family. Most likely they all died at the hands of the Nazis.

A guard sees me carry a German civilian's suitcase in a restricted area and asks if I have permission to leave the workplace. He writes down my inmate number, which almost certainly means I will be sentenced to death.

IN HITLER'S MOST
SECRET ARMS FACTORY

MY FIRST JOB in the Nordhausen factory was to clean parts for the V1 rockets. I had a twelve-hour workday, alternating from week to week between day and night shifts. I rarely saw any sunlight. Inside the mountain it was hard to know whether it was day or night. We ate once a day: a liter of soup, a quarter loaf of bread with a pat of margarine, and a slice of sausage or cheese. The food was decent, but that just made our constant hunger harder to take.

One day something happened that almost cost me my life. A German civilian wearing a long leather coat ordered me to carry his large suitcase for him. It all happened so quickly that I didn't have time to think clearly. Without giving it a second thought, I obeyed his instructions, followed behind him and dragged the suitcase. When I realized that we were heading toward the factory exit, it was too late. We had already passed an SS guard. Knowing that I could be sentenced to death for leaving the workplace, I put down the suitcase and turned around to go back.

But another guard had also seen me. He asked me where I was going and whether I had permission to leave the factory. I told him exactly what had happened, that I was merely obeying orders. But the guard didn't want to hear it. Leaving the workplace without permission was a clear violation of the rules, and he would have to report me. He wrote down my inmate number. That almost certainly meant that I would be sentenced to death.

I was terrified. I asked my foreman to explain the situation to the guard. He said that he would try to get the boss of our unit to help me, but that he couldn't promise anything. Thank goodness the boss managed to convince the guard to cross my name off the list. That basically revoked the death sentence that had just been meted out.

In Dora-Mittelbau we had to witness a mass execution. They were going to hang forty inmates who had been turned in for various disciplinary violations. Each inmate had a small stick fastened in his mouth to prevent him from screaming at or cursing his executioners. I would have been one of them if my foreman hadn't arranged to have my name crossed off the list.

In order to discourage sabotage, Heinrich Himmler, head of the SS, and Rudolf Höss, the first commander at Auschwitz, had ruled that even small misdemeanors should be punished by hanging.

A few days later—a Sunday if I remember correctly—they erected a large gallows at the inspection site and made us attend a mass execution. They were going to hang forty prisoners who had been turned in for various disciplinary violations. I would have been one of them if my boss hadn't helped me.

Every prisoner had a little stick fastened in his mouth by a piece of string tied behind his head. The idea was to keep prisoners from screaming insults at the SS executioners. I stood a dozen yards from the gallows, which looked like a huge soccer goal.

Though there were only five hooks, each one had two nooses attached to it. After being led up to the gallows, the first ten inmates climbed onto a platform a couple of feet off the ground and stood back to back in pairs. That way ten men could be executed at one time. Fifteen minutes later it was time for the next group of ten. The SS officers piled up the corpses in front of the gallows. They repeated this macabre procedure until all forty men were dead.

There was a single gallows off to the side. A man in civilian clothes walked up to it with calm dignity and pride, and was hung as well. I assumed that he was an English spy who had managed to locate the secret rocket factory before being caught.

Whenever air-raid sirens went off, I could see the bombers flash by through the trees. They flew relatively low and bombarded Nordhausen. But since the factory was dug into the mountain, it remained unharmed.

As we walked to the tunnels one morning, an Allied fighter plane flew so low that I could glimpse the pilot's face. One of the German guards threw himself to the ground and dragged an inmate down with him as a shield against bullets and shells.

The war was going so badly for the Germans that the work pace at Nordhausen slowed down day by day. At last the V1 assembly lines stood totally idle.

Sometimes they showed movies at the camp. The camp authorities announced them over the loud speakers in the barracks. Each time they said that the movies were open to everyone, with the exception of Gypsies, Russians, and other Slavic races; Jews weren't even in the running.

Nevertheless, one day at lunchtime they took all the inmates to a large room in the factory. A short dark-skinned man, probably a Gypsy, stood in the middle of the room playing opera music on his violin. The music soothed our aching souls. The melodies made such a deep

impression on me that I still remember them sixty years later. He also sang several ballads, including the one that starts off *Ich küsse Ihre Hand, Madam*. I was so moved that I couldn't hold back my tears.

After the war we found out that the Nazis had planned to kill us all at the Nordhausen factory. As the American troops approached the Harzberg Mountains, Himmler issued orders that the slave laborers were to be gassed in their underground galleries. Nobody was to come out alive from Hitler's factory for retaliatory weapons. By a quirk of fate, the order was not carried out and the inmates were taken to Bergen-Belsen.

[OPPOSITE]: *As we are on our way to work, an Allied fighter plane flies over us. One of the German guards throws himself to the ground, dragging an inmate down with him as a shield against bullets and shells.*

ON TO
BERGEN-BELSEN

ONE DAY IN late March 1945, the camp authorities received orders to evacuate us from the Dora-Mittelbau camp. Remembering what had happened the last time, we made sure to drink as much water as we could hold. Since we didn't have any containers, there was no way to take water along. And they didn't give us any food for the journey. But one of the other inmates told me that the post office in the camp was stocked with food packages intended for the Christian inmates. Out of sheer meanness, the Germans hadn't bothered to hand the packages out. Even though it was too late now to distribute the food, the post office was being guarded by the capos.

I decided to see if I could get my hands on a package. As I walked up to the post office, I was surprised to find out that quite a few other inmates were trying to storm it. Every once in a while, someone managed to grab a package and dash off with the capos at his heels. I waited until the capos had taken off after a plunderer, scurried into the post office, grabbed a mail sack, and ran back out.

I was only a few steps away when I received a terrible blow to the back of my head. My ears began to ring and stars danced before my eyes. For a moment I thought I was going to faint. I hunched up and managed to stagger on with the package clutched to my chest. Finally I made it to Herman and a group of other inmates. They formed a circle around me so that I could open the package without anyone seeing me. To my delight it turned out to contain two loaves of bread, two sponge cakes, and some apples. Herman and I took a loaf of bread each, then gave away the rest to the inmates who had shielded me. I'm quite sure that the two of us would never have survived the transfer if it hadn't been for that package.

A while later the authorities ordered us into tarpaulin-covered freight cars. It was our turn to leave Dora-Mittelbau. The journey took four or five days. Through openings in the tarpaulin, we looked out at one bombed-out city after the other. As we passed Hildesheim, I looked for an undamaged house, but there were none. Herman and I nibbled anxiously on our valuable bread supply. Since we were afraid that other inmates would rob us, we made sure not to eat at daytime. Finally the train stopped at a little station with a sign that said "Bergen." We had arrived at the Bergen-Belsen extermination camp.

Our convoy was sent to a barrack area, where they assigned us to some stone buildings. We soon realized that the camp routine we had grown used to was no longer in effect. They called us to inspection only on an irregular basis. The worst thing was that there was hardly anything to eat. At one inspection, the commanding SS officer told us that they would soon turn us over to the Red Cross. We just needed to sit tight and hold on. Everything was going to be all right. The only question was whether we would survive that long.

During the first week at Bergen-Belsen, we each received a total of one rutabaga and one beet. Herman grew weaker day by day. At last he couldn't even make it out of his cot. I was desperate to get hold of something to eat, so I snooped around everywhere I could think of.

During my wanderings through the camp, I came one day to a stone building. A large group of inmates was standing outside. Someone told me that it was an abandoned kitchen. A rumor was going around that there was a stock of potatoes in the cellar.

That was all I needed to hear. I decided right away to try to get into the cellar. With the successful raid on the Dora post office still fresh in my mind, I was hopeful that I would find something to eat.

After waiting impatiently until there were no SS officers nearby, I ducked into the cellar through a narrow air hole and landed right in the middle of a pile of potatoes. With my heart pounding, I began to stuff one potato after the other under my shirt. When there was no room left, I hoisted myself back up to the air hole. But I discovered to my horror that a man in SS boots was standing in the courtyard only a couple of feet away. Just then someone fired a volley of shots that echoed eerily off the stone walls.

I was sure that my time was up. I'd had fantastic luck, but my

As part of my continual search for something to eat, I have made my way into a potato cellar at Bergen-Belsen. After stuffing my shirt full of potatoes, I am about to climb back out through an air hole. Suddenly I discover that my escape route has been cut off by a man in SS boots.

fate had finally caught up with me. A potato cellar in Bergen-Belsen would be my death. Terror stricken, I crawled backwards and tried to make myself invisible. But apparently it didn't work; an inmate standing a little ways off signaled to me not to do anything foolhardy. I kept my eyes fixed on him. My life hung in the balance. Suddenly he motioned to me that the coast was clear.

I crept silently and cautiously out of the cellar and took off running without daring to look back. But that was the worst thing I could have done; the shirt tail slipped out of my pants and the potatoes began to roll to the ground. By this time, the SS officer had disappeared, but a group of inmates soon caught up with me. They held me down and started to snatch up the potatoes. Out of pure desperation, I began to scream for help. Of course, that was a perfectly idiotic thing to do, since nobody was going to help me. The only thing it did was make one of my assailants put both hands around my throat. I thought he was going to strangle me. I managed to gasp that they could have whatever they wanted, just as long as they let me go. He released his stranglehold, and I was able to stumble off, aching all over and without a single one of the potatoes I had risked my life for.

But instead of giving up, I searched for new ways to find food. All I cared about was saving Herman. My biggest problem was that I was scared of walking around in deserted parts of the camp. There were dead bodies scattered here and there, many of them with large pieces of flesh cut out of their thighs. Cannibalism terrified me. I was afraid that someone would knock me over the head out of desperation for something to eat. I didn't dare go back to the potato cellar—that was totally out of the question. I had to come up with another solution.

LIBERATION

ON APRIL 15, 1945, I ate leaves for the first and last time in my life. Near the barbed-wire fence around the camp were some birches that had just put out tender, pale-green leaves as large as mouse ears. When I climbed the tree and nibbled on the leaves, I discovered that they didn't taste bad at all. I thought about all the animals that live on vegetation. Maybe grass and leaves could save Herman and me from starving to death.

While I was considering tearing up grass and weeds to take back to Herman, I heard a motor coming in my direction. There was a huge clatter out on the gravel road, and suddenly a tank appeared.

I just stood there, petrified and astonished. The marks on the side of the tank were definitely not German. Following directly behind it was a loudspeaker van. It was obvious from the rasping, metallic voice that the vehicles had come from a long way off. It blared out in several languages that British troops had arrived to liberate us.

Suddenly I discovered a reserve of strength within me. Running straight to Herman, I gave him the news. We hugged each other and wept tears of joy.

But it was a long time before any real help arrived. The voice on the loud speaker had forbidden us to leave the camp; the risk of epidemic was too great. Many of the prisoners had typhoid fever. We had to stay right where we were.

The first thing the liberators gave us was a cup of sweetish liquid that tasted like the Ovomaltine my mother used to give me back home in Kolozsvar. Next they deloused us with a DDT spray. Neither Herman nor I had lice, but the treatment was required for everyone.

The Russian and Polish inmates who had any strength left began to hunt down the capos, block captains, and their lackeys. They beat to death the tormentors who couldn't escape in time. A few capos huddled up in the attic, but there were no longer any safe hiding places. The inmates discovered some of them on the roofs of the barracks and

I am so starved that I am nibbling on birch leaves when a British tank appears near the barbed-wire fence. A loudspeaker van follows directly behind the tank blaring out in several languages that we have been liberated.

flung them down to the courtyard. If they didn't die from the fall, the inmates beat them to death with cudgels as they lay on the ground. Bodies of privileged inmates were scattered all over the place.

During the wave of revenge, the inmates also went after the SS officers. The officers had to run between furious inmates. But the British troops protected them from serious abuse. They ordered the SS officers to carry the dead inmates to a mass grave. The cruelest tormentors were later sentenced to death by hanging at a trial in Lüneburg.

But the Englishmen made one big mistake. They turned over the job of guarding the liberated camp to a fully-equipped Hungarian garrison that was billeted nearby. But they didn't know that these Hungarians had fought on the side of the Germans ever since 1941, mostly on the Eastern front, and that they were real roughnecks. I was almost killed the first time I had a run-in with the Hungarians.

After liberation British soldiers order the SS to pick up the dead inmates and carry them to a mass grave. The SS officers walk around in their stocking feet. The tramp of SS boots is a thing of the past.

As usual, I was desperately trying to get some food for Herman and me. Food was still hard to get, and Herman was very weak. Finally I decided to look for something to eat in the village of Bergen, which was located a mile or so from the camp.

I squeezed through a hole in the fence and took off. Some other ex-inmates were returning with crates of groceries on their backs and gave me directions to the village. When I got to Bergen, I walked around for a long time without seeing any food. Since I was all alone, I didn't dare steal from a farm. Finally I was completely exhausted, sat down with my back to an empty shop window, and fell asleep.

I must have slept for quite a while when someone patted me on the shoulder and asked in French if I was hungry; he and his friends were about to eat. They turned out to be a dozen French officers who had been German prisoners of war. While waiting to go home, they had turned the nicest house in the village into their headquarters. As

Strange as it may seem, liberated Bergen-Belsen was guarded by Hungarian officers who fought on the side of the Germans during the war. When I return to the camp after looking for food in the village of Bergen, I am almost shot. But I escape by sounding firm and speaking German. The clothes—women's underwear and a riding outfit—have been given to me by some French officers.

they were making dinner, they had seen me sitting on the sidewalk fast asleep. When I walked into the house, they were setting the table. While the food was being prepared, I took a bath. They even ransacked the place looking for some clean clothes for me to wear.

For the first time since the morning in April 1944 when we were ordered out onto the street in Kolozsvar, I almost felt like a human being. Nobody had the right to tramp on me any longer.

After going through all the closets and drawers, the officers finally found something that would fit me: underwear and a riding outfit. They were women's clothes, but what difference did that make? Anything was better than my hated, striped prison uniform.

When the meal was over, I told them my story in German, sprinkled with a few words of French that I had picked up from some fellow inmates. They seemed to understand most of what I said. They wanted me to stay there that night, but I explained that Herman would worry about me if I didn't return until the next day. The owner of the house must have been a bicycle dealer—one room was overflowing with spare parts, but there were no rideable bicycles in sight. One of the officers began to put together a bicycle for me, while another officer took me upstairs. In the attic, slabs of smoked pork hung in long rows. He said I could have as many as I wanted. I took two. They also gave me a backpack so that I could carry them more easily. Since the camp was still patrolled by armed Hungarian soldiers, I hid the bicycle behind a bush a good ways from the fence. That way it would be easier to slip back into the camp, and I could always retrieve the bike later. But two armed Hungarian soldiers showed up just as I was trying to crawl back into the camp. I was horrified when I heard one of them say that I should be shot.

I made a quick decision to speak German—the language of "the master race"—instead of Hungarian. As firmly as possible, I said, "Wait a minute, please," opened my backpack, and took out one of the slabs of pork.

After hesitating a moment, they took the pork and waved me on.

The encounter with the Hungarian soldiers brought me back down to earth. Our lives were still hanging by a thin thread. Although we had been liberated, that was no guarantee of survival. The war offered no guarantees. Death could be lurking for us at liberated Bergen-Belsen just as easily as at Auschwitz.

PEACE IN EUROPE

ONE MORNING THE whole camp celebrated. We all hugged one another. The Englishmen danced with the female ex-inmates. Everyone laughed with joy. The war in Europe was finally over.

On May 7, the day after my seventeenth birthday, the Germans surrendered. A few days later, officials from the UNRRA (an international relief organization that gave assistance to countries devastated by war) came to Belsen and handed out clothing. It was wonderful to exchange my women's clothes for a suit. A week later the British military commanders decided to relocate all healthy inmates. We got into trucks and drove to the nearby city of Celle, where we were assigned to barracks abandoned by a cavalry regiment. Most of us had to sleep in stalls.

The Red Cross had officially classified us as survivors of the German concentration and extermination camps. Although the British allowed us to move around freely, they discouraged us from trying to go back to our countries. The railroad systems in war-torn Europe were still chaotic.

We still lived with gnawing hunger. When we found out that there was a bombed-out zwiebach toast factory on the outskirts of town, we went there right away. We cut out huge slabs of pre-mixed dough and took them to a bakery. The baker agreed to bake zwiebach for us in exchange for half of the dough. We gratefully accepted his proposal. Two days later we picked up large bags of newly-baked, delicious-smelling zwiebach.

As we began to eat regularly again, we slowly but surely recovered our strength. We each received a certain amount of money, 100 Reichsmark if I remember correctly. The Reichsmark was still valid currency, but there wasn't much we could do with the money. There was a severe shortage of all kinds of goods in Germany.

Soon they transferred us back to the barracks near Bergen-Belsen.

This time it wasn't a question of stalls, but of honest-to-goodness rooms. We shared the barracks with female ex-inmates, most of them Hungarian women who were dating British officers and so had every possible luxury. Some of my friends and I became good friends with three sisters from Hungary who were staying in the next barrack. They also wanted to go out with the Englishmen, but they were too shy, claiming that they didn't even know how to flirt. I had a sudden inspiration. "Dress me up as a girl, and I'll show you what to do," I said, half in jest. They went for my suggestion right away, and before I knew it I was dressed as a woman, makeup and everything. With a laugh, I took one sister by the arm, while the other two followed behind. We just strolled along and had a good time, and it wasn't long before two Tommys (what we called English soldiers, because of the tommy guns they carried) joined us. "See, there's nothing to it," I explained to the sisters.

Soon rumors of our stunt spread to all the barracks. The girls were yearning for some recreation. What had begun as a little game led to my being swamped by eager girls wanting me to play the role of seductive teenager. I was flattered by all the attention. We got to know another family of sisters—this time four of them, each one prettier than the last. The oldest one was dating a high-ranking English officer. She told me that he was ready to leave his wife and children if she agreed to marry him and move to England. One of my best friends fell in love at first sight with the youngest sister. But the girls had decided to go to the U.S., where some relatives were already living. It was many years before my friend got over her.

There was a movie theater in the area, but girls were allowed to attend only if accompanied by a Tommy. One of the sisters and I—in my female disguise—were invited to the movies one evening. But as soon as we got inside, we slipped away from our suitors. In the dark of the theater, staying with them was much too risky, at least in my case. Even without our dates, it was no fun. I had to spend all my time removing soldiers' hands from my thigh.

My lovesick friend and I signed up to work at the British headquarters. Since both of us could print and draw well, they assigned us to make traffic signs in English. The job gave us a number of privileges, and for the first time we felt as though we were on the way back to a normal existence. It was also a relaxing way to pass the time, and my

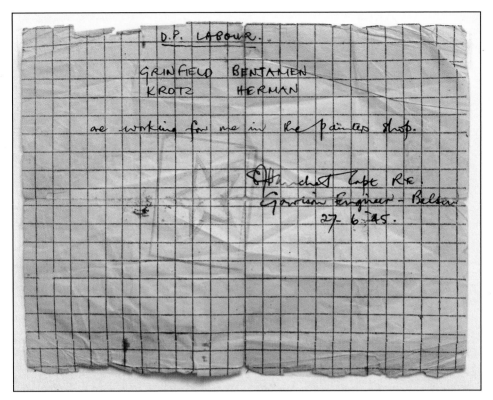

D.P. LABOUR.

GRINFIELD BENJAMIN
KROTZ HERMAN

are working for me in the painters shop.

[signature] Capt RE.
Garrison Engineer - Belsen
27-6-45.

As some Germans were about to beat me up and steal my bicycle, this little piece of paper saved me. It certi-
fied that I worked for the British.

friend had something to think about other than his unrequited love. We still keep in touch. Nowadays he's a successful manufacturer in Jerusalem, plus a proud father and grandfather.

Thanks to my work at British headquarters, I could even afford to buy a bicycle. But Germany in the spring of 1945 wasn't a place where you could wander around without endangering your life. As a friend and I rode to Celle one day, a group of Germans surrounded us. One of them claimed that my bicycle belonged to him and tried to grab it. The situation was getting out of hand. If two British military police hadn't come to our rescue, the Germans surely would have beaten us up and stolen our bikes. We took the incident as a warning that we weren't safe just because the Nazis had surrendered. Germany had sunk into total lawlessness.

After returning to the barracks at Bergen-Belsen, I came down with a severe case of dysentery. Both food and drink passed right through me. I grew weaker and weaker. At last I had to go to the local hospital. Unfortunately, all of the employees were Germans, and I was still scared to death of them. Doctors frightened me more than anyone else; I was so afraid that one of them would give me some kind of fatal injection that I hardly dared sleep at night.

The doctors had been the cruellest killers in the concentration camps. They were responsible for selecting inmates for the gas chamber. In addition, they put sick inmates to death with lethal injections containing anything from phenol to gasoline to pure air.

One day I found out that ailing ex-inmates could sign up to go to Sweden for continued treatment. The very next evening I left the hospital and got onto a train in the village of Bergen. Herman was also in our little group. When we arrived in Lübeck the next morning, German health-care workers were waiting for us. They immediately put me on a stretcher and took me by ambulance to army barracks. Large tents had been erected on the barrack square. The Germans turned us over to Swedish Red Cross personnel.

My emotions upon seeing those nurses and doctors are hard to describe. For the first time in over a year, I felt somewhat secure. I was only seventeen, but it was the happiest moment of my life.

ON TO SWEDEN

THAT EVENING THE Red Cross took us to the port of Lübeck, where a Swedish ferry called *Kronprinsessan Margareta* (*Crown Princess Margareta*) was waiting for us. We had already been disinfected, examined by the doctors, and given clean underwear. The ferry left the dock late at night. Due to lack of space, many of us had to sleep on deck. In order to keep warm, we bundled up in long Swedish military coats. It was almost impossible to sleep. Some thin crackers were all we got to eat. They tasted good, but couldn't satisfy our persistent hunger.

The sun was shining bright as we passed through the Falsterbo Canal and docked at the port of Helsingborg, Sweden. It was like arriving in heaven: a clean city untouched by the war, with friendly and helpful people. We were still plagued by images of bombed-out German cities and the incomprehensible misery of the camps.

They took us to the public baths right away. When we were finished showering, we each received a fresh change of underwear and a grayish hospital uniform. As I sat on the bus to Landskrona, I discovered suddenly that I had lost my little prayer book somewhere along the way. I still miss it today.

In Landskrona, a medium-sized coastal town in the very south of Sweden, we stayed in a vocational school that was closed for the summer. There were over 300 of us, and we represented many different nationalities. We had a wonderful matron who was like a mother to us. As Herman walked through the classrooms one day, he ran across a display case of fine tools. Immediately he went to the matron and asked to borrow a silver coin; he wanted to make a little something for her. It turned out to be a lovely brooch. She was delighted and called a local jeweler. When he said that he wanted to meet the craftsman, Herman received special permission to leave the quarantine area. The jeweler decided right away to employ him. He promised Herman that he could start as soon as his work permit was approved.

After we had stayed in Landskrona for a month, they sent us to a little camp for Romanian refugees located between Örebro and Skinnskatteberg in central Sweden.

We received 1.5 kronor (about thirty cents) each day in pocket money. We could also earn extra money felling trees in the woods. Since I wasn't strong enough yet for that kind of work, I took a job in the kitchen chopping firewood. My daily wages of 2.5 kronor was a lot of money back in 1945. But all that ended one day when I sliced off the tip of my thumb.

Herman soon got permission to work as a goldsmith for the jeweler in Landskrona. I could have gone to high school in Berga, but I wanted to stay with Herman. His employer found a job for me with a glass cutter right across the street. It was my first real job in Sweden. I earned thirty kronor (six dollars) per week.

Within a few months we wrote to our aunt in Romania. Soon afterwards she wrote back and reported that our older brother Armand had also survived the war and was in Germany. She also sent the address of our father's twin brother Jacob, who was now living in the U.S. Overjoyed by the news, I jumped onto my bike and pedaled as hard as I could to Herman's shop. Hugging each other, we jumped up and down with joy, while the jeweler stared at us with a bewildered expression on his face.

Soon afterwards we received a letter from our uncle in which he vowed to help us emigrate to the U.S. We also had a number of other relatives living there. Armand was also on his way to the U.S., so we gladly accepted the offer. But before Jacob could arrange the trip, we received a letter from his wife informing us that he had died after an operation and that she couldn't make good on his promise.

I decided to quit my job with the glass cutter in order to work in a textile factory, where the pay was a little better. Herman moved to Malmö and continued on to Stockholm after only a few months. I met Eva, a Hungarian-Jewish girl, and developed a deep attachment to her. It was not long before I realized that I was in love. One day she received a letter from her sister, who she had thought died in the concentration camps. Of course, she was overjoyed, and I was glad for her sake. But if she wanted to see her sister, she had to go to Czechoslovakia. I said good-bye to her with a heavy heart, desper-

After Herman retired from his job as a goldsmith, he got the necessary time to develop his artistic skills in other ways. In particular, he took up painting, which allowed him to express many of his inner feelings. He works both with oils and pastels, and he has had numerous exhibitions both in Sweden and in Canada, where he moved in the late 1980s.

In dealing with his demons, Herman configures the Holocaust into some of his work. The above oil painting provides one of his strongest artistic expressions of the horror experienced in the camps.

ately hoping that we wouldn't be separated for too long. Afterwards, we stayed in touch via mail for more than two years.

I was terribly lonely after she left, so I decided to move to Stockholm, where there were plenty of jobs. I found a job with a company that manufactured wire cables. The plant was conveniently located near my apartment in Sundbyberg, some eight miles away from downtown Stockholm. Around the same time, Herman opened his own jewelry business in downtown Stockholm.

IN ISRAEL,
1948–1952

I N THE SUMMER of 1948 I read in the newspaper that former Nazis had enlisted as volunteers on the Arab side in the war against the newly established state of Israel. This information aggravated me so much that I asked the Swedish Zionist Association to help me enlist as a volunteer in the war between Israel and the Arab countries. I assumed that the Israelis wanted as many soldiers as they could get. Confirming that reinforcements were sorely needed, they said that I could count on leaving within fourteen days and that they would soon contact me with further details.

The notice of departure came more quickly than I had expected. Though I had an alien's passport, which wasn't valid for re-entry into Sweden, I didn't plan to stay in Israel forever. I would have preferred not to leave without permission to re-enter, but there was no time to arrange it. However, the Zionist Association promised to take care of my re-entry when the time came. Everything was ready to go. Several of my friends joined me, including one with whom I had made traffic signs for the English at Bergen-Belsen. We were thrilled to see each other again. We took the train from Stockholm to Malmö, then flew from Bulltofta to Amsterdam. Israel had bought an old passenger liner from Holland and re-christened it the *Negbah*. We weren't scheduled to leave for Israel until a week later. With my meager savings, I bought a round-trip ticket to Brussels, where Eva was living with her sister and some other relatives. It was a happy time for me. But that only made it that much more painful when I had to say good-bye and return to Amsterdam. The voyage to the Israeli port of Haifa took over a week.

I now became one of roughly 3,500 *Machalniks* (*Machals* for short)—*Mitnadvei Chutz L'Aretz*, to use the Hebrew term, and Volunteers from Outside Israel, to use the English translation—that came into Israel and fought alongside Israel's regular armed forces.

When a flurry of press photographers greeted us, we were all flattered, until we discovered that they had come to take pictures of the ocean liner. We took a bus to a military base on the outskirts of Haifa. The war was going full steam, and the city was blacked out. The next day we went to a large military base further south and received our uniforms. Several days later we went to Tel-Litvinski for training. I was assigned to the Air Force along with one of my friends from Sweden. After a few days at headquarters in Jaffa, we went to an air base near Rehovot, where we joined a crew comprised of several different nationalities. Most of the technicians came from the U.S., England, Sweden, and South Africa. A while later, a whole contingent of Italian technicians arrived. My commander was a big, jovial American.

During WWII, the airstrip where we worked had been a base for Liberator bombers. After bombing missions, they returned to base seriously damaged. Most of them ended up helter-skelter in one big pile. Plucking parts from the plane wreckage was not an entirely safe thing to do. Our job was to construct a workshop for overhauling aircraft engines accessories. We built test benches, and also performed a complete inspection of the accessory parts, which we finally repainted and tested. The most difficult job was building a test bench for the Stromberg fuel-injection carburetor. When, after a great deal of effort, we had almost finished the construction, a completed test bench arrived from the U.S.

Certain spare parts were difficult to get hold of. One episode I particularly remember involved the booster pumps (electrically-powered gasoline pumps which insured that the motor-powered gasoline pumps always had enough fuel, regardless of the plane's position in the air) for the Spitfire attack plane; the pumps were hard to get into working condition. After a complete overhaul and subsequent testing, it turned out that they leaked. The leakage was caused by a deficient rubber seal on a metal washer. Before long the Spitfire flights had to be suspended due to a lack of adequate booster pumps. When I was at a nearby office one day, I noticed a secretary typing stencils. Whenever a key went through the stencil, she would replenish it with some kind of sealing wax. That gave me an idea. I asked if I could borrow her little bottle of sealing wax for a while. I tried it on one of the rubber seals. To my great delight I succeeded in fixing the leak. Soon we had functional booster pumps and the attack planes could fly again.

New types of planes were constantly being developed. The Israelis bought everything they could get their hands on. Before long we had to expand both staff and facilities. I made friends with a number of Swedish pilots, mechanics, and other specialists. A few of them played an important role in my life after my return to Sweden, including a legendary pilot by the name of Thorvald Andersson, who started an airline where I worked long afterwards. I got along just fine in the Israeli Air Force. I learned English, a little Hebrew, and even some aircraft mechanics.

I was discharged from military duty after a year and a half. I agreed to stay on as a civilian mechanic, but soon began to long for Sweden. In addition, I suffered from sciatica. I applied for a re-entry visa at the embassy, but it was turned down. Then I wrote to the enlistment office in Stockholm reminding them of their promise to help me return to Sweden. The promise turned out to be worthless. Herman was my last resort. He contacted the Aliens Commission, the forerunner to today's Immigration Board. Though I had never done anything illegal during my stay in Sweden, they refused my application over and over again. At last Herman requested an appointment with a prominent member of the commission. They let him speak with an assistant. Herman explained that we had miraculously survived the war, lost our whole family, and felt that we had to be together. Otherwise he would close down his shop and leave Sweden. Apparently that impressed the official, because he promised to seek approval of my application at the next meeting of the commission. It took a year and a half for me to obtain permission to return.

Herman sent me tickets for the boat from Haifa to Marseilles and for the train from Marseilles to Stockholm. I longed to see Paris. Since I had read so much about the city, it was fantastic actually to be there. I stayed a little over a week. That was all I could afford. On the train from Paris to Copenhagen, I ate the cheapest meals; soon my money ran out completely. I was very hungry, so the trip from Copenhagen to Stockholm was quite a trying experience. Somewhere along the way a group of Swedish teenagers began to unwrap the snacks they had brought along. My mouth watered and I tried to look the other way. But one of the girls asked me if I wanted to join them. I gratefully accepted some bread and butter. It felt as if I were returning to a warm-hearted family. Unfortunately, I was too shy to ask for her address and telephone number. I would have liked to return her kindness.

In 1998 I was invited to Jerusalem along with all other surviving *Machals* by the Israeli President Ezer Weizman. On May 4, 1998, in connection with the celebration of the fiftieth anniversary of Israel's statehood, I was decorated by the President for my services as a *Machal* in the war of independence.

THE MIRACLE
OF OUR SURVIVAL

ERMAN AND I had survived the camps. Instead of our ashes being wafted out through the chimney, we had walked out on our own two feet. At first we believed that we were the only members of our family who had not been killed. We learned later that our brother Armand was alive as well. But everyone else was gone.

Just like us, they had been taken by train to Hitler's most horrible extermination camp. With a wave of his hand, a doctor in impeccable uniform had decided our fates right then and there: you to the right, you to the left. . . .

It was nothing less than a miracle that both Herman and I survived. Most of the prisoners were sent to the gas chamber during the first or second elimination rounds. It was an even greater miracle that I came out alive after being sentenced to death three times.

Reading the historian Martin Gilbert's book *Auschwitz and the Allies* (New York: Holt, Rinehart, and Winston, 1981) provides even more precise evidence how minute the probability of our survival was. Gilbert reports that the first train from Hungary to Auschwitz-Birkenau arrived on May 17, 1944. As with later deportations, the train consisted of forty sealed freight cars with 100 Jews in each one. It went directly into the camp on the newly-built side track, stopping only a few yards from the gas chambers. Only seventeen men out of a total of 4,000 passengers went to the barracks; the rest were gassed. The second train arrived on May 18. Of the more than 4,000 passengers, all were gassed except for twenty women. On May 19 all the new arrivals were gassed except for seven men. From the train that arrived on May 20 (probably ours), thirty-four men and fifty-eight women were selected for slave labor, while the rest were gassed. All told, over 16,000 Hungarian Jews were murdered during this four-day period. In other words, not even 1 percent of the deportees survived the very first elimination round.

I would estimate that the chances of staying alive in Auschwitz and the other camps for as long as we did were about 1 in 100. In addition, fifty percent of the inmates died during the train ride to Dora. Taking all these factors into consideration, I would say that my chances of survival were approximately 1 in 20,000. The probability that my brother and I both would survive and live through Auschwitz, Dora-Mittelbau, and Bergen-Belsen was so tiny that it was almost non-existent. But somehow it happened.

AFTERWORD

SIXTY-ONE YEARS HAVE passed since the day that British tank came rattling up the road to Bergen-Belsen to announce that the war, as well as our captivity, was coming to an end. As a retiree I can finally devote myself to my hobbies, particularly painting, which has always been my strongest interest.

I have always known that I wanted to write down and relate my experiences in the German extermination camps. As early as 1947, I began to write down my experiences, but I gave up. It was too painful and anxiety-ridden. I did not realize then that Nazism would once again rear its ugly ahead around the world—even in Russia, the country that lost 20 million people as a result of Nazi barbarity.

I haven't been able to forget all the horrors I have seen; for better or worse, I have been gifted with a photographic memory. Hardly a day has passed that I have not thought about the Holocaust. When I bought my house in Kallinge, I seriously considered building an emergency exit or a hiding place, in case I was ever in danger again because of my Jewish background.

During a vacation in the Canary Islands, my wife and I celebrated New Year's Eve with some good friends. Right in the middle of all the festivities, I suddenly remembered my father, who never allowed himself a single week of vacation, simply slaved and toiled his whole life in order to support his family, and thought about myself in contrast. I pretended that I had a headache and left the party.

As long as I had my career to fall back on, I could hold my memories at bay. After retirement, they inevitably popped up again. I got very angry in the early 1990s when I saw an interview on Swedish TV with a sixteen-year-old boy who said that he could shoot a black person without blinking an eye. Incidents like that have reinforced my conviction that I have a responsibility to recount what happened to me. Also, due to the rise of the Neo-Nazis and the attention that the "revisionist" movement (a movement under the leadership of

Frenchman Robert Faurisson, who claims that the Nazi genocide of the Jews never took place) has received, that desire has turned into a sense of duty.

When we studied history in school, I always shuddered at the cruelties that man had committed against his fellow human beings. I consoled myself with the thought that such cruelty was no longer possible in the civilized world in which I grew up. But how mistaken I was! What is even more deplorable is that people are still committing genocide today, more than sixty years after Auschwitz. With all the knowledge we possess of earlier misdeeds, how could we permit what happened in ex-Yugoslavia during the 1990s? Don't we ever learn anything from history? My personal answer to that question is that man is never going to win an ultimate victory over evil. The struggle has to continue forever. The day we sit back and believe that evil has finally been conquered, you can be sure that danger will be lurking just around the corner.

I spend a great deal of time going around to schools and relating my experiences during the Holocaust. In recent years I have given roughly 100 talks per year about my Holocaust experience. That gives me a great deal of inner satisfaction. I feel as though I am the mouthpiece for all the unfortunate people who were killed just because they happened to have been born Jewish.

Benny Grünfeld
Kallinge, Sweden
Summer 2006

THE HOLOCAUST

AN HISTORICAL BACKGROUND *BY OLLE HÄGER*

THIRTEEN-YEAR-OLD ANNE FRANK was the author of the most widely-read diary from the Nazi era. An Amsterdam family hid her from her persecutors for two years, but finally the Nazis discovered her and took her to concentration camps in Germany.

She died of typhus and malnutrition in March 1945 at the Bergen-Belsen camp.

One week later, sixteen-year-old Benny Grünfeld arrived at the same camp. He was so famished that he ate birch leaves to relieve his hunger.

On April 15, 1945, the first Allied tanks rolled into the camp. For Benny and his fellow inmates, the long imprisonment in death's shadow had come to an end.

If Benny had died as the Nazis planned, the ashes of his emaciated body would have been shovelled out of the crematorium at Auschwitz-Birkenau and mixed with those of hundreds of thousands of other inmates. After all, that's what the Holocaust was all about.

But, in defiance of both evil and death, he survived.

Someone has calculated that a third of the world's Jews died in the Nazis' camps. But it was neither the first nor the last time that Jews have been the victims of persecution and terror.

Anti-Semitism, or hatred of Jews, has a long history in Europe. Early Christian theologians argued that Jews had brought misery and suffering upon themselves by refusing to believe in Jesus.

During the Middle Ages Jews were excluded from European social life. In addition, they were admitted to only a handful of professions, among them money lending.

The conditions of Western European Jewry improved somewhat in the eighteenth century, but Jews have been treated with distrust long into our own time.

HITLER'S RISE TO POWER

Adolf Hitler, who was elected German Chancellor in 1933, used anti-Semitism as a political weapon. He and his Nazi followers did not hesitate to blame all of Germany's problems on the Jews. One of the first things he did was order the construction of concentration camps.

The official purpose of the 1935 Nuremberg Laws was "to protect the purity of the German race." The laws forbade Jews to marry non-Jews and took away their citizenship, including the right to vote. Hitler tried to force them to emigrate. And half of them did leave Germany, many after having been the victims of brutal abuse.

In November 1938, on what has become known as *Kristallnacht*, synagogues were burned and Jewish homes and businesses were looted throughout Germany.

But it wasn't easy for Jewish refugees to find countries willing to take them. In 1939 Swedish students successfully stopped the immigration of a handful of Jewish physicians.

"Protest against the import of Jews." In February 1939 students in Stockholm, Uppsala, and Lund successfully stopped the immigration of a handful of German-Jewish physicians who were seeking work and asylum in Sweden.

CONCENTRATION CAMPS FOR JEWS AND PRISONERS OF WAR

After Germany invaded Poland in September 1939 and the Second World War broke out, the Germans built new concentration camps one after the other. The camps were no longer primarily for Germans who opposed Hitler, but for prisoners of war, Jews, Gypsies, and other "undesirables."

Before long the Germans forbade Jews to emigrate from Germany and other countries that Hitler had seized in the war. In addition, they required each Jew to wear a yellow Star of David as a mark of identification. Polish Jews had to live in patrolled ghettoes.

Germany's invasion of the Soviet Union in 1941 marked the beginning of the mass murder of Jews. Special German commands followed

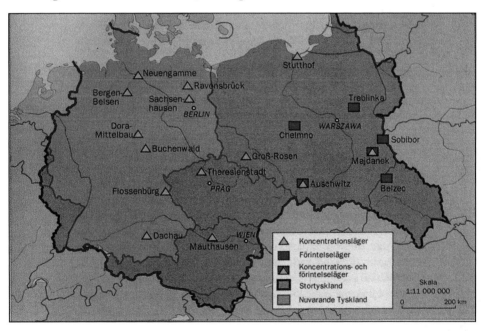

The map shows where the major Nazi concentration and extermination camps were located. Dachau, the first concentration camp, was set up as early as 1933. During the Second World War, additional camps were constructed one after the other. Eventually there were over 500 of them. Most of them were for slave laborers, who were used to man the German war industries.

While the Nazis cold-bloodedly and methodically killed millions of Jews and Gypsies in the extermination camps, hundreds of thousands of other inmates died of exhaustion and illness in the labor camps.

Translation for key above (from top to bottom): Concentration camps; Extermination camps; Concentration and extermination camps; "Greater Germany"; Germany today.

at the heels of the troops and killed every Jew they could lay their hands on. Women as well as men, from old people to little children, were thrown onto the backs of trucks and driven to out-of-the-way places, where they were shot and shoveled into mass graves.

The worst blood bath occurred in Babi Jar, near the Ukrainian city of Kiev. In a matter of just two days, more than 30,000 Jews were killed.

Soon the executioners turned to poison gas. At the beginning, they simply let carbon monoxide back up into covered trucks. But eventually the Belzec, Sobibor, and Treblinka extermination camps were built; Jews were deported there from all over Poland, then killed in specially-designed gas chambers.

THE AUSCHWITZ EXTERMINATION CAMP IN POLAND

The Germans began the construction of Auschwitz, the largest camp of all, during the summer of 1940 around abandoned military barracks not far from the city of Katowice in southern Poland. A year later they expanded it to include the gigantic Birkenau camp, which eventually consisted of over 300 buildings. In 1942 they put the Monowitz labor camp into operation. That is where Benny Grünfeld spent most of his time, working as a slave laborer at the I.G. Farben chemical plant.

Thousands of inmates were brought to Auschwitz from all over German-occupied Europe. Most of them arrived by train. At that point they had traveled for weeks, confined to overflowing freight cars under the most dreadful conditions imaginable.

Their fate was decided as soon as they stepped onto the platform. The Nazis chose a few of the strongest ones to perform slave labor. But they sent most of the inmates directly to the gas chambers and crematoria.

Auschwitz-Birkenau was basically an extermination camp, a death factory. Its crematoria could burn more than 8,000 bodies per day.

The mass executions normally occurred in the gas chambers. The Nazis led hundreds of inmates at a time into the room under the pretense that they were about to take a shower. Then they leaked Zyklon B, a deadly poison consisting of hydrocyanic acid in crys-

A mass grave for inmates at the Dora-Mittelbau concentration camp near the German city of Nordhausen.

talline form, into the sealed chamber; within a few minutes, all the inmates were dead. Afterwards the Nazis removed gold fillings and cut off women's hair, which was used to weave cloth for garments for military personnel working in particularly moist environments such as submarines. Finally, they took all the bodies to the crematorium ovens in the same building.

"THE FINAL SOLUTION"

The overall planning for the Holocaust occurred at a meeting in Wannsee on the outskirts of Berlin in January 1942. Some of Germany's highest officials were there. The minutes of the meeting refer to "the final solution of the Jewish question." That was the Nazis' euphemism for one of the most elaborately designed genocides in human history.

There is no way to determine exactly how many people were killed at Auschwitz-Birkenau. Most of them went directly to the gas chambers without being identified or counted. Historians have concluded that the figure is somewhere between 1.3 and 1.5 million.

All in all, the Nazis killed between 4 and 6 million inmates. The great majority were Jews, but other groups that the Nazis had decided to exterminate were also represented, among them Gypsies and homosexuals.

In the summer of 1944, when Benny Grünfeld was at Auschwitz, more inmates died each day than at any other time. Most of them were Hungarian Jews.

The efforts of Raoul Wallenberg, a Swedish diplomat in Hungary, led to the rescue of thousands of Hungarian Jews, particularly in the Budapest area. But over 400,000 of them were deported to Auschwitz anyway. One of them was Benny Grünfeld.

HOW COULD THE HOLOCAUST HAPPEN?

All of the German concentration camps, extermination camps, and labor camps were administered and patrolled by officers of the SS, a special unit under the command of Heinrich Himmler, the hard-boiled chief of the Gestapo secret police.

In what came to be known as the White Buses, the Swedish Red Cross rescued many Danish and Norwegian inmates, whom the Germans had imprisoned after occupying their countries, from the German concentration camps.

A few of the SS officers and guards were sadistic madmen and unscrupulous brutes. But most were ordinary soldiers. Nevertheless, they participated willingly in one of history's most horrible atrocities.

The fact that such a thing could happen was closely linked to the efficiency with which the Holocaust was designed. Everything was organized down to the last detail and carried out one step at a time.

It all began with Hitler's idea of purging Germany of the Jews. The final result was that millions of Jews were murdered.

The gap between Hitler's vague ambition and the actual Holocaust was bridged by thousands of bureaucratic tasks and decisions, each one relatively innocent in itself. Evil proceeded step by step.

Some barbed wire was delivered, grating was ordered for a crematorium oven, a timetable was adjusted, a conductor drove his train to Auschwitz, a crate of poison gas was picked and taken to a specified storage location in a barrack—all according to official orders.

Viewed as a whole, the thousands of bureaucratic measures constituted an invincible death machine. No evil madmen were needed in order for it to function. Indifference was all that was required, since violence—in the form of simple duty and routine—was built into the very system.

During the final stage of the war, the Germans tried to wipe out all traces of what they had done. They destroyed crematoria and burned down barracks.

As the Soviet Red Army approached, the Germans forced the inmates to march westward. It was the middle of winter and many thousands died.

Only the hardiest inmates could even start off on this march. They were the ones who had survived the constant threat of death in the labor camps. A few of them finally ended up in Sweden, where they had a chance to rebuild their lives.

SOME IMPORTANT DATES

1920—The German National Socialist Party is founded. Its members call themselves Nazis. Adolf Hitler is chosen as party leader. Anti-Semitism is one of their major planks.

1933—Hitler assumes power in Germany. Books written by Jews are burned in public bonfires. Jews are excluded from government service. Jewish physicians are boycotted and forced to close their practices.

1935—The Nuremberg Laws strip German Jews of their civil rights. Marriage between Jews and "Aryans" is forbidden.

1938—On November 9, *Kristallnacht*, Jewish homes and businesses are destroyed and hundreds of synagogues are burned down. Tens of thousands of Jews are taken to concentration camps.

1939—Hitler invades Poland on September 1, marking the beginning of the Second World War.

1942—At the Wannsee Conference on January 20, the elimination of European Jewry is laid out. One extermination camp after another is constructed in Poland.

1945—Germany surrenders on May 7. The Nazi camps are opened, and the world sees for the first time the extent of the catastrophe the Jews have suffered.

GLOSSARY OF TERMS

Anti-Semitism: animosity toward Jews, a prejudice with a long history in Europe. At the beginning anti-Semitism was based on religion. Accused of having killed Christ, Jews were excluded from European social life and restricted to a few professions.

In the nineteenth century an ideology of anti-Semitism emerged. The "Jewish race" was portrayed as inferior to the "Aryan race," to which such peoples as the Germans and Swedes were said to belong.

Arrowcross: the Hungarian Nazis. Szálasi, their leader, formed a government in late 1944 that cooperated with the Nazis in their persecution of Hungarian Jews.

Aryans: employed properly, this term refers to all people who speak one of the Indo-European languages. The Nazis, on the other hand, used it in opposition to the "Semites," i.e., such peoples as the Arabs and Jews, who were considered to belong to the lowest of all races.

Capo: a concentration camp inmate who was put in charge of his fellow inmates by the administration of the camp.

Concentration camps: at the beginning, they were labor camps for criminals and political opponents of the Nazis. During the Second World War, prisoners of war, homosexuals, Jehovah's Witnesses, Gypsies, and, above all, Jews were sent to the camps.

Nearly half of the inmates died of starvation, illness, or inhuman treatment.

Deportation: the act of being imprisoned and sent away, for example to a concentration camp.

Extermination camps: camps built by the Nazis for the express purpose of carrying out mass murder. First constructed in 1941, they were all located in Poland. Auschwitz and Treblinka were the most infamous.

Gestapo: the Nazis' secret police force that employed terror to quash dissent in Germany and the areas it occupied. Its chief was Heinrich Himmler.

Ghetto: an enclosed residential area to which a group of people is restricted. The first Jewish ghetto was set up in 1516 in the Ghetto quarter of Venice.

Hitler Youth: a Nazi youth organization.

Holocaust: the systematic genocide of the Jews at the hands of the Nazis during the Second World War.

Jewish Star: see *Star of David*.

Jews: initially referred to those who inhabited the ancient kingdom of Judah, but which later came to designate those who practiced the Jewish religion.

Fr The Nazis believed that there was such a thing as a Jewish race, but were unable to discover any biological evidence of its existence. So they simply defined a Jew as anyone whose grandparents had belonged to a Jewish congregation.

Kristallnacht: the night of November 9, 1938. The Nazis organized a nation-wide attack on Jewish shops and synagogues. Over thirty Jews were murdered and more than 20,000 sent to concentration camps.

Nazism: an abbreviation for National Socialism, a political movement that asserted among other things that certain people (the "Aryans") were superior to others (for example, Muslims and Jews).

Founded in 1920, the German National Socialist party was run almost single-handedly by Adolf Hitler. Elected German Chancellor in 1933, he eventually appointed himself as dictator.

Nazism is closely related to Fascism.

Nuremberg Laws: anti-Semitic German laws promulgated in 1935 in the city of Nuremberg. Jews were stripped of German citizenship, and marriage between Jews and "Aryans" was outlawed.

Pogrom: attack on minority groups, especially Jews; usually a mob action instigated by government authorities.

Selection: the process by which ill or feeble concentration camp inmates no longer capable of performing slave labor were chosen for elimination, i.e., death.

SS: abbreviation for the German *Schutz-Staffeln*, the Nazi "defense groups." The SS was comprised of the SD secret service, the Waffen-SS combat units, and the units in charge of the concentration and extermination camps. The black-uniformed SS units were under the command of the infamous Heinrich Himmler.

Star of David: a six-pointed star that has long been a symbol of Judaism, for example on the Israeli flag. In Nazi-dominated Europe, Jews were forced to wear a yellow Star of David—what the Nazis called a "Jewish Star"—sewed on their outdoor clothes.

Torah: the Five Books of Moses, written by hand on a parchment scroll bound to a pair of wooden poles.

Zyklon B: a lethal agent consisting of hydrocyanic acid in crystalline form, used in the gas chambers of the extermination camps.

ABOUT THE AUTHORS

BENNY GRÜNFELD was born in 1928 in Cluj (or Kolozvar, in Hungarian) in what is today Romania. After miraculously surviving the Holocaust, he and his brother Herman arrived in Sweden in mid-July 1945. To be able to remain with his brother Benny turned down an offer to enter senior high school and instead became a blue-collar worker, first working for a glass cutter and then in a factory.

After three years in Sweden, first in Landskrona and then in Stockholm, Benny enlisted as a volunteer in the Israeli Armed Forces and participated in the Arab-Israeli War. In Israel he was trained as an aircraft mechanic. After four years in Israel he returned to Sweden and, by virtue of the skills he had acquired in Israel, managed to get a job in Sweden's then-budding civil aviation industry. Between 1952 and 1962 he lived and worked in Stockholm. From 1962 until his retirement in 1993, he was employed at the Kallinge air field outside Ronneby in southern Sweden.

After his retirement Benny began visiting schools in order to relate his experiences during the Holocaust, and since then has travelled to schools throughout the country. In fact, this soon grew into a second career, and in recent years he has given roughly 100 talks a year in school auditoriums across Sweden, reaching out to some 10,000 high school student every year. Given that an age cohort in Sweden is around 100,000, this number is substantial.

Benny obtained his pilot's license in 1958, and throughout the 1960s flying was one of his favourite hobbies. It was also during this period that he took up painting. He paints in oil, and he finds his inspiration outdoors, mostly in landscapes. Benny has had many exhibitions in the province of Blekinge where he lives.

Benny is married to Solveig and they have three children together. He also has eleven grandchildren.

MAGNUS HENREKSON was born in 1958. In November 1956, at age nineteen, his biological mother Gabriella Zador (b. Palfy, 1937–2006) escaped Hungary following the Soviet invasion. After a short interim in an Austrian refugee camp she came to Sweden in early 1957. She became pregnant later that year, and rather than opting for a life as a single mother in a foreign country she decided to give up her child. As a result, Magnus grew up as an adopted child in a Swedish farming family. He knew from an early age that he was adopted and that his biological mother was Hungarian.

He first met his biological mother in 1984, and it took several years before she told him who his biological father was. Gabriella's first years in Sweden had been tumultuous and the pregnancy was the result of a brief relationship. The father had never been informed of the pregnancy, let alone the birth of his son. Magnus contacted his biological father Benny Grünfeld in 1992, and they began to make up for time lost. Benny retired a year later, and, partly as a way of getting to know each other, they compiled Benny's memories from the Holocaust years into a book manuscript.

Very early on Magnus showed talent for academic studies and had a vivid interest in social matters. He eventually specialized in economics. After receiving his Ph.D. in 1990 he has been an academic economist. In Sweden he is a well-known and respected academic, and for almost twenty years he has been a keen and frequent controversial participant in the Swedish public debate. He is currently Jacob Wallenberg Professor of Economics at the Stockholm School of Economics and President of the Research Institute of Industrial Economics in Stockholm. In his research he has covered a wide array of topics, but in recent years his main interest has been the role of entrepreneurship for economic development and prosperity.

Magnus is married to Karin and has two daughters, Ebba and Hedvig, born in 1992 and 1994, respectively.

OLLE HÄGER was born in 1935. He grew up on a small homestead in Hälsingland, a province in the center of Sweden dominated by forest land and forestry. Olle broke away from his background and enrolled at Uppsala University, where he studied humanities. His academic studies were completed when he defended his dissertation in history dealing with the authenticity of the accounts of the life and deeds of the Swedish king Gustav Vasa in the 16th century. Since 1964 he has been a radio and television producer. He has specialized in historical documentaries, and he has received numerous national and international awards for his films. The government of Sweden awarded him an honorary professorship, a highly prestigious and rare award, in 1996 for his achievements.

His work as a documentary filmmaker has been the object of academic examination in a recent Ph.D. dissertation: David Ludvigsson (2003), *The Historian-Filmmaker's Dilemma: Historical Documentaries in Sweden in the Era of Häger and Villius* (Department of History, Uppsala University).

Olle is also an author of books. He has published ten historical books and several crime novels. At age seventy-one he still works as a documentary filmmaker at the Swedish Public Service Broadcaster—Sveriges Television (SVT).

During his work with Benny's Holocaust memoir, Magnus contacted Olle, who found the story so compelling that he wanted to make a film based on it. The film, entitled *A Round Trip to Hell—with Benny Grünfeld in Auschwitz*, was first aired in 1996, and has since then been shown numerous times in Sweden and several other countries. Olle also became involved in the book manuscript. In particular, he wrote the historical background to Benny's highly personal account.